MIRRORS

MIRRORS

SERGE ROCHE

GERMAIN COURAGE

PIERRE DEVINOY

RIZZOLI
NEW YORK

Translated by COLIN DUCKWORTH and ANGUS MUNRO

First published in the United States of America in 1985 by
RIZZOLI INTERNATIONAL PUBLICATIONS, INC.
597 Fifth Avenue, New York, NY 10017

Library of Congress Cataloging in Publication Data

Roche, Serge.
    Mirrors.

    Translation of: Miroirs, galeries et cabinets de glaces.
    Bibliography: p. 320
    1. Mirrors – History. 2. Decoration and ornament –
History. I. Courage, Germain. II. Devinoy, Pierre.
III. Title.
NK8440.R613   1985   749'.3   85–2055
ISBN 0-8478-0605-7

Printed and bound in Germany

Contents

Editor's Foreword

Over the past number of years there has been a growing demand for a well-documented book on the subject of mirrors, in response to the new interest in mirrors as collector's pieces and ornaments, as distinct from their function as pieces for furniture. In each epoch and culture within the history of mankind the magic world of mirrors has produced unique forms and styles, and for this reason the historical development of the mirror cannot be described solely in terms of the frames or interior decoration, but instead requires to be studied in its own right.

With this book we wish to present an enlarged edition of Serge Roche's "Miroirs – Galéries et Cabinets de glace" which was published in Paris in 1956 by Paul Hartmann and which is almost impossible to obtain nowadays. A large part of the black-and-white illustrations by the late Pierre Devinoy have been retained, but the entire colour section has been recast. By way of contrast to the first edition, both the text and the illustrations have been supplemented with striking examples of mirrors from the Art Nouveau and Art Deco periods since these two movements have had an important effect on mirror design in the 20th century.

Serge Roche was for a long time the leading expert on mirrors in France and his gallery in the Rue St. Honoré (now the Galérie Jacques Kugel) was a centre where designers, art lovers and leading buyers from all over the world gathered. In 1934 an exhibition was held in his gallery under the patronage of M. François Carnot, the president of the Union Centrale des Arts Décoratifs. This exhibition with no less than 92 antique mirrors attracted much attention at the time and has remained to this day unsurpassed in both range and quality. Serge Roche was at the same time, however, himself a creative mirror designer whose work was sought after by international dealers. His introduction to this work spans varying epochs and cultures, and the author illustrated his descriptive text with a fascinating series of literary quotations.

Using burning-mirrors Archimedes sets fire to the Roman fleet attacking Syracuse. Portrayal from Vitellio's works on Optics (Book V) written approx. 1270 and published by Risner 1572.

Preface

It is now twenty-five years since, in *French and Foreign Frames*, a classification of picture-frames was undertaken. In this new panorama the history of the mirror and its frame is described and illustrated. The halls of mirrors and mirror rooms which were so popular in the seventeenth and eigteenth centuries are also shown.

The mirror is certainly one of the oldest of all accessories. Intrigued by his reflection in water, Man tried to perpetuate this miraculous phenomenon, using a variety of materials to record the fleeting image. This preoccupation spread gradually throughout the whole world, and for forty centuries artists and artisans contrived, like alchemists, to give to bronze, silver, gold, tin, steel, iron pyrites, volcanic glass (obsidian), and rock-crystal the wonderful qualities of calm water. After all these experiments, it was Venice, the most magical of all cities, which saw the birth of two new techniques which made crystalline and blown glass possible. Once the materials had been invented, all that remained to be achieved was the elaboration of an endless variety of frames. The fabulous world of the mirror was created.

CHAPTER ONE

Antiquity

The round mirror discovered in the course of excavations at Susa, the capital of ancient Elam, may be the original of the type of mirror found in Egypt, Greece, Etruria, in Scythian regions, Persia and China. Many beautiful specimens of bronze hand-mirrors, with handles sometimes of ivory, bear witness to the importance of this small requisite in ancient Egypt — the Cairo Museum has one dating from the twentieth century B.C. Scythian bronze mirrors from the sixth century B.C. have been found in the Caucasus. The Hebrews, who learnt the use of them from the Egyptians, possessed so many of them that Moses was able to make for the tabernacle 'the laver of brass, and the foot of it of brass, of the looking-glasses of the women assembling at the door of the tabernacle' (Exodus, 38.8). The Chinese have handed down to us mirrors of bronze and platinized or silvered bronze. From as far back as the Three Kingdoms and the Ch'in dynasty we find them either round, square, or in two parts folding into one another, one of the two pieces often being pierced. Inscriptions appear on some; one of them, for example, reads 'Great Joy, Honour, and Riches'. The backs are sometimes damascened in gold or silver or studded with turquoises. The traditional kind of workmanship continues throughout the Han and T'ang dynasties. The Louvre has a large number of Greek mirrors in bronze and silver (Ills. 9–11, 13).

Many Etruscan mirrors been found in tombs, decorated on reverse with finde outline drawings of amatory mythological subjects. On one Etruscan tomb (in the Archaeological Museum, Florence) a dead woman is shown looking in her mirror. The Vatican Museum has an Etruscan hand-mirror dating from the sixth century B.C. The Romans followed the Greek tradition and made mirrors of tin at Brindisi (Buffon). In one of the murals at Pompeii, Cupid is holding a mirror for a woman doing her hair, and mirrors figure in two more of these murals which are kept in the Naples Museum.

It is said that Demosthenes practised his speeches before a large mirror. These articles abounded in Rome and were an essential toilet-requisite for every woman of fashion. Seneca mentions full-length metal mirrors, and also notes that they cost more than it takes to provide a general's daughter with a dowry. The so-called 'mirror of Virgil' (a transparent, oval object about a foot across, and an inch thick) used to be kept in the treasury at Saint-Denis.

The scientific importance of the mirror soon became apparent. Euclid laid the foundations of optics, and particularly catoptrics, in the third century B.C., then Ptolemy and Hero of Alexandria developed his principles. In the Middle Ages the Arab Alhazen (about 1200) and Vitellio (about 1270) made further contributions to the science of reflected light. The work of these mathematicians made all kinds of mirrors possible — flat, curved (concave and convex), burning and magic mirrors in various geometrical shapes (ellipses columns, pyramids).

The Greeks lit the sacred fire of Vesta by capturing the sun's rays with a concave vase of gold. Archimedes is supposed to have set fire to the Roman fleet attacking Syracuse, with the aid of a burning-mirror. Ptolemy II (283–247 B.C.) built at Pharos a tower upon which he installed a mirror that enabled him to see enemy ships sixty miles out to sea. And it was not with stones, but with a mirror, that Prometheus created fire.

CHAPTER TWO
The Middle Ages

The popularity of the mirror up to the end of the sixteenth century only serves to confirm these very ancient examples. From the thirteenth century onwards mirrors of burnished metal (imitation classical style) are to be found beside mirrors of rock-crystal and of glass backed with a sheet of silver or lead. The term 'crystalline glass' appears for the first time in the inventory of René d'Anjou, in 1448. Skilful glassmakers of Murano (Andrea and Domenico are mentioned in 1516) were already making 'good and perfect mirrors of crystalline glass'.

From the beginning of the sixteenth century the 'city of lagoons' boasted of being able to supply the world with silvered blown glass mirrors of fine quality, and these were being manufactured in Germany and Flanders at the same period. In France attempts were made to use crystalline glass at the manufactory of Mathieu Carpel in Lyons. Henri II tried to introduce the new glass-blowing industry into France. Letters patent were given by the king on 13th February 1551 'granting to *sieur* Theseo Mutio, an Italian gentleman born in "Boullogne" the exclusive grace and privilege of making or having made within ten years and in this Kingdom mirrors in the fashion of Venice'. But his glasshouse did not live up to expectations. The glasshouses established later in Lorraine gained great reputation, but not until the second half of the seventeenth century did France and England offer any effective competition to Italy.

The mirrors made in Europe during the Middle Ages, whether of metal, crystalline glass or blown glass, were all small. They can be classified in several categories:

(*a*) Mirrors for pocket, dressing-case, and girdle. Very valuable articles, popular until the seventeenth century; fitted into boxes of metal, leather or carved ivory, attached by a fine chain, also often worn in purses hanging at the side. The ivory cases were often decorated with courtly subjects (the first meeting, the amorous conversation, the rendezvous, the declaration, the lover triumphant), or romanesque ones — Tristan and Isolde, for example (the water of a brook, at the foot of a tree, revealing to them the reflection of King Mark who has climbed the tree to spy on them). Poetic allegories are also represented (the fountain of Youth, the siege of the castle of Love, the heart's profferment), as well as purely religious or pious subjects (the Adoration of the Magi, etc.). Several fourteenth and fifteenth century examples are preserved in the Louvre and the Cluny Museum (Ills. 35–41).

There are also some sixteenth century pocket-mirrors in Limoges enamel on exhibition at the Louvre; we reproduce several of them (Ills. 50 and 51). A small Italian girdle-mirror figured in the collection of Mme de Jubinal de Saint-Albin during the nineteenth century, its ivory case bearing the inscription: 'Complain not of me, O Woman, for I return to you only what you give me'. It came from the house of Leonardo da Vinci. On another pocket-mirror from the same collection, in silver and silver-gilt, were the following mottoes: 'To be together or to die', 'Sweetness beguiles me', 'To see you or die', 'Indifference drives me away'. The Landau collection has a small silver-gilt pocket-mirror made in Augsburg about 1600; the back of translucent enamel is decorated with an intaglio of cornelian.

(b) Toilet or standing-mirrors (imitation classical style). The earliest types are those represented in the 'Lady with the Unicorn' tapestry, now in the Cluny Museum (Color Plate II), and in the tapestry of the Apocalypse in Angers cathedral, woven about 1375. A specimen in damascened iron is to be seen in the Victoria and Albert Museum. In the 'Cabinet d'un Amateur' exhibition at the Orangerie in 1956, item No. 286 was an octagonal table-mirror on a stand of chased bronze, with reverse side églomisé (painted and gilded,) made in the late sixteenth century (Ill. 211). An ivory standing-mirror made in Munich by Christoph Angermeier during the last years of the sixteenth century appears in the A. Lopez Willshaw collection (Ills. 117 and 118). A portrait presumed to be of Diana de Poitiers, in the Dijon Museum, shows a curious table-mirror decorated with pearls and supported by bronze figures. So we see how the standing-mirror, which used to be held up by a servant before the master or mistress, came soon to be placed on a table; the foot or stand was replaced by a mermaid of silver-gilt holding a crystal mirror, and then by a support (valet) or stem which allowed the mirror to be inclined at any chosen angle. The inventory of Catherine de Medici mentions one of the latter kind. The sixteenth century also sees the birth of the toilet-case. Among the purchases of François I in 1538 was a toilet-case described as having 'scissors and brushes of Mauresque design, covered with fine gold and close-set with rubies and turquoises, and a small mirror similarly wrought'.

(*c*) Hand-mirrors, also inspired by antiquity and usually executed in ivory (see ill. 42). The Cluny Museum has a curious wooden comb with two compartments containing small mirrors protected by sliding-doors (Ill. 41). Damascened steel hand-mirrors are reproduced in ill. 47.

Numerous examples of hand and pocket-mirrors are to be found in the engravings of sixteenth century ornamentalists. Among the designs for small mirrors by Jacques Androuet Du Cerceau is one decorated with chimeras and warlike subjects in the centre, and another with coupled columns surmounted by a pediment. In the note-books of Etienne Delaune (called Stephanus) there appear eight designs for hand-mirrors with wrought gold ornamentation, and in another volume six designs for square, round and oval hand-mirrors (see Ill. 44–46). A small mirror, scroll-shaped, decorated with pinked leather and figures, is to be found in the work of Pierre Wœriot. A very curious piece, attributed to Benvenuto Cellini, represents a mermaid holding a comb in one hand and a small mirror in the other. A large baroque pearl forms the mermaid's body, the head, arms and tail being of translucent enamel on gold, decorated with rubies and topaz. It was presented to a Mongolian emperor of India by one of the Medicis (Ills. 209 and 210).

The popularity of these precious mirrors in steel, gold, silver, tin, rock-crystal and crystalline glass can be judged from their frequent recurrence in inventories:

(i) Steel mirrors are mentioned in 1317 in the accounts of the silver-smith of Philippe le Long, and in 1380 in the inventory of Charles V. The inventory of the Crown jewels in 1418 records 'a large steel mirror with the coats of arms of France and Bourbon'. François I bought five in 1532 from the jeweller Guillaume Hotman, and four more large ones in 1534 from Allard Plomyer. In the inventory of Charles-Quint, in 1536, one reads: 'A large mirror in steel of ancient style embellished with small pearls and closing with two shutters (clouans)'. At the close of the sixteenth century, the inventory of Henry VIII of England lists steel mirrors with carved wood frames polychromed or decorated with velvet embroidered with pearls and gems. The Victoria and Albert Museum possesses Italian Renaissance mirrors with carved walnut frames ornamented with scrolls and masks, the steel reflecting-plates being protected from oxidization by curtains or removable pictures. A mirror with carved wood frame and shutter is kept at the Museé des Arts Décoratifs in Paris (Ill. 48).

(ii) Gold mirrors are listed in the inventory of Louis I, Duke of Anjou in 1360, and in that of Charles V in 1380 there is mention of 'a mirror garnished with pearls'. Among the large number of pieces of jewellery claimed for the Crown of England as having belonged to Isabelle of France (1400) was a mirror of gold 'shaped like a daisy'. King René paid the German silversmith, Hennequin, twenty *écus s'or* for supplying a gold mirror which he presented to the wife of the Seneschal of Anjou as a

New Year's gift. The inventory of Gabrielle d'Estrées records in 1599 'a mirror all of gold, in the centre of which is an agate with two figures carved in relief thereon, and a portrait of the King in the said mirror which is garnished with diamonds and rubies and with heads in relief upon an agate enamelled red'.

(iii) Silver mirrors are mentioned comparatively rarely: two occur in inventory of Clemence of Hungary in 1328, the one enamelled, the other in an ivory case. Charles V's inventory (1380) lists 'a large silver mirror with the arms of Queen Jehanne of Bourbon and on the back a picture of Our Lady'. In the inventory of Fançoise of Brittany (1481) we read of two silver mirrors 'in two lobster-shells adorned with amber'; in that of Charlotte of Savoy (1483) a silver mirror mounted in an amber brush. And the secret expense accounts of François I record that in 1538 he bought from Allard Plomyer 'a large mirror of silver-gilt enriched with divers stones and feathers'.

(iv) Crystalline glass mirrors appear at the beginning of the fifteenth century and continue until the end of the sixteenth. In his description of the Abbey of Thélème, Rabelais remarks that 'in each backchamber there was a crystalline mirror set in a frame of finde gold, garnished all about with pearls, and of such proportions that it would represent to the full all the lineaments of the person that stood before it'. François I was a great purchaser of crystal and crystalline glass mirrors, paying four *écus d'or* to Guillaume Castillon in 1529 for 'two gold-plated apples serving to hold perfume, and within, two little books containing the seven psalms, and two mirrors at the sides'. In 1532 Allard Plomyer supplied a crystal mirror garnished with gold and precious stones. In 1533 Jehan Grain supplied thirteen, and in 1538 Jehan Grespin, Loys Poucher and Allard Plomyer supplied seventeen mirrors of which one was of 'crystal set in carved damascened ebony', and another 'of crystalline covered with velvet and enriched with embroidery'.

One of the most famous mirrors of this period is that of Maria de Medici, now exhibited in the Galerie d'Apollon at the Louvre. It is described minutely in the inventory of Crown furniture:

'A mirror of architectural design, with frontispiece in sardonyx, in the centre of which is a head of Diana in a similar agate, surrounded with emeralds; on each side a small vase in sardonyx; the cornice resting on two columns of grey jasper, supported by two pilasters. In the cornice-frieze are twelve heads on mounted emeralds separated from one another by three small emeralds; beside the columns, two heads of garnet with gold enamel embellishment on two large emeralds also with gold enamel embellishment; in the centre of the pedestal, a woman's head surrounded with emeralds; all on gilded copper and standing upon six small round balls of sardonyx, the size being about fifteen inches tall down the middle by ten inches wide.' (Colour Plate III).

I. Mirror box in carved lacquer. China.
Ming Dynasty (1522–1575).

II. Tapestry entitled "The Lady and the Unicorn". France. 15th c.

III.   Mirror of Maria de Medici. Italy. 16th c.

IV. Peter Paul Rubens. "The Toilet of Venus". 1610–1620.

"Picture of a beautiful and well-shaped lady".
Copper engraving by Paulus Fürst. Late 16th c.

A mirror of damascened iron adorned with figures is to be seen at the Petit Palais Museum (Ill. 204). At the Cluny Museum are an octagonal mirror in gesso, marble and bronze (Ill. 207), and an architectural frame in gesso and lapis lazuli. At the Figdor sale in Vienna in 1930 there was a round mirror in faience adorned with angels' heads created by Della Robbia in the fifteenth century. Mirrors for the populace were usually of tin and were sold by travelling pedlars.

Curved mirrors. Burning-mirrors, convex or concave, made by cutting a sphere in two halves, were first produced during the Middle Ages. Distorting mirrors were one of the attractions at the château of Hesdin (Pas-de-Calais) in the fifteenth century. Colard the Robber, the Duke of Burgundy's valet, who was put in charge of arranging the decoration of a great hall, fixed in the entrance 'a mirror in which are seen divers illusions', that is to say, in which people saw distorted reflections of themselves. In the inventory of the Duke of Lorraine, in 1543, at the château of Nancy, these is mention of 'a strange mirror in which one sees another rather than oneself'. Curved mirrors are also to be found frequently in bed-boards and in physical laboratories. Rabelais says they were used by practical jokers sometimes 'to annoy people and make them lose countenance at church'.

Magic mirrors. These were already in use in ancient times, and constituted part of the sorcerer's paraphernalia in the Middle Ages. In the *Sorcerers' Demonomania* (Paris 1580) Bodin quotes Pausanias: 'If anyone wished to know whether he would recover from his illness, he put a mirror in the Fountain of Patras before the Temple of Ceres; if he saw in it a man full of life, he would recover'. These mirrors revealed occult and secret things; Simon Goulart, in his *Treasury of Admirable Stories* (Vol. 4 of the 1610 edition) describes a magic mirror scene which took place in the château of Chaumont-sur-Loire: 'The Marshaline of Raiz has been heard to say that Queen Catherine de Medici, wishing to know what would happen to her children and who would succeed them, summoned someone to assure her on the matter; he had the children shown to him in a mirror representing a room round which each one walked as many times as he would reign in years. King Henry III, having taken his turn, was followed by the Duke of Guise who crossed it like a streak of lightning, and the Prince of Navarre who took 22 turns about the "room" and disappeared incontinent.' An engraving depicting this scene was pusblished in 1710, and appears in Marana's *Spy of the Great Lord*.

J.-B. della Porta speaks, in 1589, of distorting mirrors — spherical (concave and convex), elliptical, pyramidal and cylindrical — which divide the face in two parts, make it look like a donkey's nose, a pig's snout, or a dog's head, and make the eyes stand out like a crab's. The same author also mentions the theatrical mirror, that is, a set of mirrors forming a polygon within a circle, and speaks of a casket with its inside con-

17

trived in this way, which so multiplies a few jewels placed in it that one would think one were looking at the most splendid treasure in the world.

In 1663 J.-F. Niceron reveals that those who describe themselves as soothsayers, sorcerers or magicians with the power of making anything appear that they want, merely use these mirrors and are in fact nothing but imposters.

Mention must also be made of the death-mirrors, on the bottom of which was a death's-head, expressive of sorrow at the death of someone dear; and the mourning-mirrors, painted or enamelled black, which women wore at their waist when in mourning. Catherine de Medici ordered one from the silversmith Du Jardin in 1572 to give to the Queen of Navarre.

Leonardo da Vinci considered mirrors could instruct the artist: 'When you wish to see if your picture is exactly like the real thing, take a mirror, reflect the living model in it, and compare this reflection with your work — and see how near the original is to the copy'. Leonardo's manuscripts are frequently in mirror-writing.

The mirror is referred to in the litanies of the Virgin (or of Notre-Dame de Lorette) laid down by the Fathers of the Church at the Council of Ephesus in 431 ('The Mirror of Justice'), and angels are often compared to mirrors because of their perfection and purity. Nevertheless, a mirror in the hands of a woman has, since the beginning of Christianity, been considered a symbol of sin. In the Middle Ages, the Church seems to proscribe the use of the mirror, held to be an object of vanity and lust. The Bull of Pope John XXII (1326) affirms that 'the Devil can conceal himself in a phial or a mirror'. Lust is represented by numerous statues, and on stained-glass windows (for example, the rose-window of Notre-Dame in Paris), as a court lady holding a mirror as an emblem. But what are we to think of the fifteenth century miniature in which a lady is selling burning-mirrors to a monk (MS. of the *Pilgrimage of Human Life*, in the British Museum)! The severity of the Church towards mirrors becomes attenuated with time; altars are decorated with them in St. Philip's, Palermo; the Church of the Jesuits, Salamanca; the Church of St. Joseph, Seville, and in Lisbon Museum; and mirrors adorn a throne in the Church of Vichs in Germany. In the chapel of Andechs, near Munich, and in the church of Zwiefalten, small pieces of mirror are set in the vaults which are decorated with rococo stucco work (Ills. 165 and 166). It is significant that whilst in Flanders, mirror-markers were sometimes ranked with painters, in France the corporation of mirror-makers joined in 1581 with that of the toy-makers.

Mirror with frame in coral, white enamel and gilt bronze. Naples. Late 16th c. Octagonal frame 0.55 × 0.35 m. Pierre Delbée Collection.

CHAPTER THREE
Europe, 17th and 18th centuries

1. Glasshouses

The close of the sixteenth century sees the gradual disappearance of mirrors made out of precious metal, steel and rock-crystal, as well as the more modest ones of tin and copper used by lower middle classes. The art of mirror-making was revolutionized by the Venetian discoveries of crystalline glass and of glass obtained by blowing it into cylinders. The glasshouses of Murano enjoyed a veritable monopoly and received nearly all the orders in Europe right up to the end of the seventeenth century. This new process marks the beginning of a new era in the evolution of precious mirrors. As it became possible to manufacture mirror plate in larger and larger size, the mirror ceased to be a mere trinket or a toilet requisite place upon a table; it became a means of decoration, hung on the wall like a picture. The invention of plate glass brought about a complete transformation in the form and ornamentation of mirrors. Competition was set up to counteract Italian monopoly; the glasshouses of the Low Countries, Saxony and Nuremberg, hitherto little more than branches of Venetian houses, stepped up production. Soon, in 1618, Sir Robert Mansell obtained a patent from the King of England; his connections with Venice had enabled him to bring back Venetians banished from their country. In Scotland, a glasshouse was established under the direction of Leonardo Michellini, 'a Venetian of low birth and a thorough rascal', according to the chronicles. After a few setbacks, both financial and technical (the use of coal for heating, instead of wood as in other countries, caused numerous faults in the glass), England was finally acclaimed in 1663 (the date of the founding of the Vauxhall plate glasshouse by George Villiers, second Duke of Buckingham) to be supreme in the manufacture of glass. The Vauxhall glasshouse was to be eclipsed, at the beginning of the eighteenth century, by the Bear Garden glasshouse at Bankside, Southwark.

In France, the experiments of the sixteenth century had been abortive, and the glass industry was not really created there until 1665. The honour of liberating France from the heavy tribute hitherto paid to Venice by the luxury-loving court goes to Colbert, the brilliant and indefatigable minister of Louis XIV. As a result of a privilege granted by the King to Nicolas du Noyer, a glasshouse employing two hundred workers was established in the *faubourg* Saint-Antoine in Paris. The King had the right to a discount of thirty per cent on the official tariff. This 'Company for making glass of large and small volume' was soon having to compete with the glasshouse of Tourlaville which, about 1670, under the direction of Richard Lucas, *sieur* of Nehou, exploited the method of glass casting invented by Bernard Perrot, a glassmaker from Orléans. This new technique, which is still used to this day, brought about a revolution in the glass industry and made great developments possible. Another privilege was granted to Pierre de Bagneux in 1683, who established a branch at Lézinnes (Yonne), on the estate of Louvois, Louis XIV's war minister. Then Thévart, protected by Louvois, set himself up in 1688 at La Grenouillère (now the Gare d'Orsay), to exploit Perrot's invention. In 1693 Thévart's 'Large plate glass Company' was established at Saint-Gobain, among the ruins of the old château; only the grinding and polishing was left to be done in Paris. After various financial difficulties, the different companies were amalgamated in 1695 to form the 'Royal Glass Manufactory of France', under the direction of François Plastier. Another company was founded in 1702 and Antoine Dagincourt obtained letters patent for thirty years. The company's direction passed through several hands until, in 1789 (4th August), all privileges were abolished.

2. Techniques

The two methods of manufacture in the seventeenth and eighteenth centuries were those of blown glass and cast glass. Charles de Brosses (called Le Président de Brosses), author of some racy *Letters on Italy*, gave a detailed description of the Venetian method in a letter to M. de Blancey (29 th August 1739):

'I have just returned from Murano, where I have been to see the glass-house. The glass plates are not as large nor as white as ours, but they are more transparent and less faulty. They are not cast on copper tables like ours, but blown like bottles. The work demands extremely large and robust workers, especially to swing in the air those great globes of crystal on the end of the blow-pipe. The worker takes from the crucible of the furnace a large quantity of molten matter, which is then of a gluey consistency, on the end of his pipe. By blowing he makes a hollow globe, then by swinging it in the air and putting it every now and then into the mouth of the furnace so as to maintain a certain degree of fusion, still turning it very quickly so that the matter does not run more on to one side than another, he succeeds in making a long oval of it. Then another worker with the point of a pair of scissors like sheep-shears (that is to say, they open when the hand is relaxed) pierces the end of the oval. The first worker holding the pipe turns it very quickly, whilst the second gradually opens the scissors. In this way the oval is completely opened up at one end. Then it is detached from the first iron pipe and sealed again at the open end, on to another specially made pipe. Then it is opened at the other end, using the same method I have just described. You have then a long cylinder of glass, of wide diameter. Still being turned, it is put once more into the mouth of the furnace to soften it a little again, and when it comes out, in a trice it has been cut lengthwise with shears and laid out on a copper table. After that, it only has to be heated again in another oven, polished, and silvered in the ordinary way.'

In the *Travels of a Frenchman in Italy* (1765–1766) there is a note on the glasshouse at Murano:

'The Arts are cultivated more in Venice than in the rest of Italy. The glassware of Murano goes everywhere, only that of France is considered preferable. The only glasshouse on the island of Murano is that of Giovanni Mota. They work only two days a week there, and the dozen or so workers employed are enough to blow 600 pieces of glass in a morning. The frit is made of ash from Spain and earth from Vicenza, baked in a separate oven for six hours, and this frit, placed in another crucible for seven or eight days, serves to make the glass. The blow glass four and a half feet across each way, but usually it is only three feet at the most. After blowing the plate-glass with great effort, they cut it and lay it on a stone, then with an iron shovel they put it at an inclined angle over the furnace to cool gradually.

The French method of casting consists of spreading the molten matter as evenly as possible over perfectly smooth metal tables. Then, whilst the paste is still malleable, it is marvered (rolled). So that the glass thus formed shall be suitably solid, it must cool by degrees, and to do this it is placed in a red-hot oven which is allowed to cool slowly. When the cooling process is complete, the glass is removed for grinding, polishing and silvering.

Silvering or tinning consists of laying on a perfectly smooth table of iron or marble a sheet of beaten tin the size of the glass. This tin is covered with a thin layer of mercury, and on top of this is laid the plate of glass, which has been previously polished with emery.

Mirror-glass remained expensive for a long time — which did not prevent the King from spending 376,000 livres on very lavish plate mirrors between 1667 and 1695.

One can see at Fontainebleau a small mirror set in the panelling, which is claimed to have been presented to Maria de Medici by the Republic of Venice on the occasion of the birth of Louis XIII. The fact that this mirror was mounted in the panelling shows the importance that was attached to it. An idea of prices can be obtained from Saint-Simon's amusing story about the Countess of Fiesco: 'Ah, Countess', her friends said to her, 'where did you get that from?' She replied: 'I had some wretched land which brought me nothing but wheat, so I sold it and bought this fine mirror. A mirror instead of wheat — have I not been very clever?'

3. Ornamentalists, Inventories, Gifts, Paintings, Engravings, Literature

Thus, the mirror plate that we know in our own times has been invented (except that silver is now used instead of mercury), its methods of production established, and glasshouses have sprung up in many European countries. The reflecting plate is next surrounded by frames of infinite variety; mirror-frames are ready to entertain the freest and most sumptuous suggestions in design the ornamentalists can imagine.

Etchings, by ornamentalists, inventories, lists of royal gifts, items appearing in museums, churches, and private collections, paintings and prints, and finally literature; all these enable us to establish a rough classification of the infinite variety of mirrors produced in Europe during the seventeenth and eighteenth centuries. This classification is relatively easy for France and England, where the power of the King favoured the creation of a more or less homogeneous style for each period. On the other hand, in Italy and Germany the absence of a central authority and the multiplicity of reigning princes necessitate classification by regions.

(a) *France, Seventeenth Century.* After 1620, France endeavoured to abolish from its mirror-frames the architectural style, which had originated in Italy. The Louis XIII style shows an outstanding freedom from foreign influences, and it is surprising to find even in the second half of the seventeenth century a design by Charles le Brun for a mirror bearing the King's arms, of the purest Renaissance style (Louvre). Many mirrors were still imported from Venice; the inventory of Mazarin, for example, lists in 1653 'a large Venetian mirror in an ebony moulding overlaid with German silver pierced in the form of foliage, with iron rings, hooks, and a hanging-cord of floss silk, the said mirror in a wooden box.' Mazarin had an immense collection of very beautiful mirrors of extreme richness; Louis-Henri de Loménie, Count of Brienne, asks in his mémoires 'how many mirrors garnished with gold and silver plate, carved tortoise-shell, and

ivory fashioned by excellent carvers, how many plated with silver-gilt?...'
Among the curios in the same collection was a small concave magnifying-glass in a moulding frame. The *Gazette de France* reports that at a ball given at the Hôtel de Chevreuse on the 19th February 1633 in the Queen's presence, 'the six rooms of this magnificent mansion were lined with silver mirrors'. Several types of mirror were created at this period: frames were made of carved gilt wood, adorned with fruit, flowers, or pea-pods; pediments were embellished with angels playing instruments; carving became full in outline, gilding highly burnished; or else the frame (with receding section) was laid with ebony, whalebone and tortoise-shell on red, green, or gold-leaf, the mouldings usually being guilloched.

Small mirrors still formed a part of feminine dress. The elegance of costume in the first half of the century consisted in the various accessories which enjoyed great favour with the women: fans, jewels, and all the ornaments hung from the girdle — mirror, comfit-box, watch in enamelled gold, purse of satin or velvet, and toilet-case.

Some fine designs for mirrors (in particular overmantel mirrors) have been left by ornamentalists, who became more numerous after 1650; we may mention particularly Jean Lepautre (1618–1682), Paul Androuet Du Cerceau (productive during the second half of the century), Jean Bérain (1638–1711), the architect Pierretz, F. de Poilly (1622–1693), André-Charles Boulle (1642–1732), and Daniel Marot. The mirrors with frames of carved gilt wood which we reproduce reflect the styles invented in the seventeenth century, particularly those by Lepautre, Bérain, Boulle and Marot.

Beside this purely French production, constituting the Louis XIV style, the King in his inexhaustible artistic curiosity bought from foreign dealers 'Venetian mirrors set in crystal, German mirrors with flaps and frames embellished with coloured crystal and agates'. The general inventory of Crown furniture (1663–1715) was made by Gédéon du Metz, who, as general controller of Crown furniture, was made responsible by Louis XIV for 'providing for the security and preservation of *objets d'art.*' This important document gives us very valuable information regarding the technique of framing mirrors, of which almost five hundred are described, many of whose borders are recorded as being of white, blue, green and flame-coloured glass embedded in mouldings of silver-gilt, Spanish or German white silver, gilded copper or filigree of German silver. Other frames in the royal collections were of burnished steel, 'imitation lapis', tortoise-shell, agate, ebonized pear-wood, walnut, cedar, kingswood, and wood the colour of calambar. From the end of the seventeenth century, carved gilt wood is largely used, oak, sage, laurel and vine being the foliage motifs. One border of rock-crystal mounted on damascened gilt wood is mentioned, as well as numerous mirror plates with belleved edges and frames, candlestick brackets and sconces in chased silver.

Mirrors, for the most part of lavish design, were made for Versailles, Trianon, Marly, the Tuileries, Chambord and Fontainebleau. Even in a grotto in the Ménagerie at Versailles there were mirrors; even Louis XIV's coach was adorned with them in 1672.

Of all these treasures, little remains. Versailles Museum contains not a single mirror, and most of those set in the panelling (apart from those in the room of the King and Queen and the great hall of mirrors), were sold at the time of the Revolution and replaced in the reign of Louis-Philippe.

Kings were not only great collectors; they also gave magnificent gifts, to members of their family, sovereign princes, titled families on the occasion of a wedding, and ambassadors; many of these gifts were mirrors which are mentioned in the archives of the French Ministry of Foreign Affairs. Sully, the great minister of Henri IV, notes that among the gifts he presented to the Queen of England when he was ambassador there was 'one of the largest and most beautiful Venetian mirrors ever seen, with a frame of gold covered with diamonds'. In 1666 Louis XIV gave a silver-gilt toilet-case to the King of Sweden, and one to the King of Norway. In the same year he gave a large mirror to the Electress of Brandenburg; in 1670 a silver-gilt toilet-case to the Queen of Poland; in 1675 a large mirror with silver frame to the King of Poland; in 1680 a silver-gilt toilet-case valued at 6,800 livres to the dauphine; in 1681, several burning-mirrors to the Kings of Siam and Tonkin; in the same year, a silver toilet-case worth 4,800 livres to the Electress of Brandenburg; and in 1684 'five mirrors of rock-crystal with borders artistically wrought and garnished with stones' to the King of Siam.

Charles II of England, in 1672, gave to Frances Teresa Stuart, Duchess of Richmond and Lennox, a toilet-case referred to as the 'Lennoxlove toilet-service'. This case was a masterpiece of French craftsmanship and comprised seventeen silver-gilt pieces bearing the hall-mark of Vincent Fortier (1672–1677), in a chest of oak faced with *repoussé* gilt copper. The Edinburg Museum acquired it at a sale at Sotheby's on 25th February 1954.

Burning-mirrors adorned the physical laboratories of the seventeenth century. In 1685 M. de la Garouste, a gentleman of Saint-Céré, constructed for the Academy a large burning-mirror, which this society needed in order to find out the precise effects of the sun on such a mirror. We reproduce (Ills. 53 and 54) six small round mirrors (convex) framed in ebonized pear-wood; their irregular curvature causes various distortions of image.

"Enseigne de Gersaint". Engraving by Pierre Aveline after the painting by Watteau (1684–1721). A large Louis XIV mirror, a lacquered dressing mirror and a vanity-case with mirror can all be made out on the picture. Cabinet des Estampes, Musée Carnavalet, Paris.

(b) *France, Eighteenth Century*. Ornamentalists were now becoming more and more interested in the mirror, and made innumerable designs for frames, particularly in gilt carved wood. The architect Robert de Cotte (1656–1735) is attributed with the invention of the low overmantel surmounted by a mirror instead of the paintings and bas-reliefs to be found during the second half of the seventeenth century. Among his etchings are sheets of designs for large mirror-frames.

Nicolas Pineau (d. 1754), at one time architect to Peter the Great and inventor of the rococo style, planned chimney-pieces panelled with mirrors and with pier-glasses. Jean Mariette (1654–1743), Gilles-Marie Oppenord (1672–1742) and Leroux (1676–1745) devoted several volumes to fashionable chimney-pieces with mirrors. Briseux (1680–1754) printed etchings for mirror-borders in *The Art of Building Country Houses*. Other ornamentalists who designed mirror-frames and pier-glasses were J. A. Meissonier (1693–1750), François Cuvilliés (1698–1768), Jacques-François Blondel (1705–1774), author of *The Arrangement of Country Houses and the Decoration of Buildings in General*, Thomas Germain (1673–1748), J.-C. Delafosse (b. 1721), Boucher fils, de Lalonde, Salembier, and Prieur.

Under the influence of these masters, carving became extremely varied. New types of mirror-frames were created. At the beginning of the century, they were rectangular with mirrored panels *(parecloses)* attached by hooks of carved gilt, wood, and surmounted by a strongly marked pediment. During the *Régence* period (1715–1723) the *parecloses* disappeared into the arched pediment and made one with it. Decoration featured fantastic animals, winged griffons, monsters, and palms.

During the Louis XV period, the *parecloses* tended to disappear, leaving only the gilt moulding. Woodcarvers were able to avoid destroying the linear rhythm, despite the indentations, swirls, and asymmetrical forms which the ornamentalists incorporated in their designs. The rococo style brought its formulary of coquillages, undulations, branches and foliated scrolls. Chinese influence began to make itself felt at the same time. Platinum, and gold in various shades (red, green, lemon) were used. So long as glass could not be made in large plates, mirrors were made in two parts, the division usually beingt two-thirds of the way up. Towards the middle of the century, a period when the trade of carver and of gilder became more and more secure, a new style was created. The mirror-frame became rectangular again, Greek corners were developed, pediments were enriched with vases or trophies joined to the frame by garlands of flowers. Imitation classical moulding was adorned with ova, pearls or water-leaf. We reproduce several types of these eighteenth-century mirrors, which have been preserved more particularly, in France, in private collections.

The royal chronicle mentions a mirror belonging to Louis XV, 'a beautiful mirror with borders and caps of glass with blue ground, the upright borders being in the form of pilasters draped with vine-shoots, leaves and grapes of white glass. The upper border is a frieze, slashed and foliated, also of white glass; the lower one is adorned with cornucopiae, the scrolled cap with swags of leaves and flowers, and the King's cypher in a festoon of oak-leaves, crested with a royal crown, the whole in white glass.

One of Louis XV's toilet-mirrors was 'arched and scrolled above, garnished all over with yellow damask and with two silver bands, the support similarly garnished'. When the King visited the curio-room of M. Pajot d'Ours in Bray, he was shown 'an excellent burning-mirror valued at 25,000 livres, which dissolves all sorts of metals. The King had the pleasure of watching a *louis d'or* and several pieces of steel being melted'.

In the eighteenth century, kings gave away sumptuous mirrors as presents; to Sultan Mahmoud I went, in 1742, 'two large mirrors 15 feet by 8 feet with a border of bronze, cast and chased by Caffieri after a design by Gabriel, representing the attributes of the Ottoman Empire, trophies, and the treasures of the sea', valued at 24,982 livres. In 1751, several mirrors made at the royal manufactory at Saint-Gobain were given to the King of Denmark, to a value of 24,576 livres. The minor expenses account of the King reveals that the mirror-maker La Roue supplied a jewellery cabinet to the Countess of Provence in 1770. Among the articles given to the Count of Choiseul-Gouffier (the King's ambassador to the Sublime Porte) to be distributed in His Majesty's name to the great Ottoman ruler, his ministers and principal officers, on the occasion of his Highness's first audiences, there figures ... a mirror with border (3,005 livres). See also ills. 63, 64, 68, 73, 75 and 78).

Silversmiths achieved some magnificent toilet-cases in the eighteenth century. The exhibition of 'French Art in the 18th Century' at Copenhagen in 1935, contained a toilet-service with mirror (Louis XV period) bearing the arms of the Duke of Cadoval; it was made in 1739 (see Ill. 72). A large silver toilet-mirror by F. T. Germain used to be kept at the Grand Palace of Peterhof, in Russia. Item No. 35 at the S. R.[1] exhibition of 1934 was a dressing table mirror forming part of a toilet-service by Imlin of Strasbourg, dated 1775, with the arms of Hesse-Cassel (J. Helft collection). We have noticed in a private collection a silver-gilt mirror with armorial pediment, which came from a toilet-case of the Louis XVI period and was made by Kirsten in Strasbourg. (See also Ills. 70, 80 and 86.)

Etiquette demanded make-up, so much so that all ladies had in their pocket a box containing patches, brush, and mirror. The patch-box in Ill. 79 belonged to the Marchioness of Pompadour, and was made in 1759 under the supervision of Richard. Another patchbox, gold, Louis XVI period, is to be seen in the 'Au Vieux Paris' collection. These precious

[1] S.R. — Serge Roche; the author's exhibitions are abbreviated thus throughout.

boxes recall the nine positions for patches, each denoting that the woman is passionate, majestic, vivacious, wanton, caressing, forward, flirtatious, discreet, or light-fingered.

In the realm of science, the eighteenth century saw the invention of the mirror microscope. Loewenhoek's microscope (1690) was simply a spy-glass.

During the reigns of Louis XV and XVI appear several types of furniture with mirror: the toilet-table, the heart-shaped dressing-table, then the escritoire and the *barbière*.

Before the war, at the inauguration of an exhibition, Anatole de Monzie asked who had been the first to invent the mirror-wardrobe; at that time we did not know that the beautiful Mme de La Popelinière, wife of the farmer-general, had one made to conceal a secret communicating door leading to the house of the Duke de Richelieu.

(*c*) *Germany*. Germany, like Flanders, was one of the first countries to make mirrors of crystalline glass, and established glasshouses as soon as glass-blowing had been discovered by the Venetians.

The main ornamentalists who designed mirror-borders were, in the sixteenth century: Dietterlin (1550–1599) creator of the style often used in the façades of Bavarian castles at the close of the sixteenth century; Unteutsch, who worked about 1650 and spread throughout Germany the auricular style of the Dutchman Lutma; Johann Ulrich Stapff, of Augsburg, who designed for the silversmiths frames richly ornamented with carved foliage and amorini.

Decker (1677–1713) of Nuremberg, adopted the themes of Daniel Marot. One of his works, published at Augsburg in 1711, mentions 'a room of curved distorting mirrors, a kind of comical joke' (Ill. 132). Albrecht Biller, of Augsburg (1663–1730) designed frames adorned with lightly-marked, much-pierced foliage reminiscent of Chippendale style.

In the eighteenth century, Franz Xavier Habermann (1721–1796) produced for the silversmiths of Augsburg designs in rococo style; and at the close of the century, J. M. Hoppenhaupt, C. A. Grossman, J. Grodman and J. Hauer designed frames for mirrors and pier-glasses.

The Germans used a wide variety of materials for mirror-frames: amber in Dresden, cut crystal in Bohemia, silver and silver-gilt in Augsburg, ivory in Munich.

The following are a few characteristic examples of various techniques: a small amber box with mirror on back of lid (No. 19 at the S. R. exhibition, 1934), typical of the large number of articles made of this substance which are kept in the Dresden Museum; there is in the Serge Roche collection a mirror with frame of fine guilloched gilt mouldings, and inner border covered with small pieces of Bohemian glass faceted like diamonds, separated by silver braid (Ills. 123 and 124); in the Berlin Museum, an oval mirror with frame of carved ivory incrusted with shell and hard stones, surmounted by an eagle and the Kurbrandenburg arms on the pediment; the Kunstgewerbemuseum in Munich possesses a mirror in a monumental frame enriched with cartouches, figures and death's-heads (late sixteenth century), and a dressing-table mirror in a rococo frame of repoussé silver; item No. 306 in the 'Chefs-d'œuvre de la curiosité du monde' exhibition at the Pavilion de Marsan in 1954, was one of the most richly ornamented mirrors ever produced in Germany: it is of silver, silver-gilt and shell, and was made in Augsburg in 1700; the Hanover Museum has a very interesting toilet-case in enamel, made in Berlin; the inventory of the Imperial Russian palaces lists a toilet-case in gold with mirror, bearing the arms of the Empress of Russia, and made in Augsburg (1730) by the silversmith Johann Ludwig Biller.

(d) *England.* At the close of the sixteenth century, Quen Elizabeth used, for her toilet, mirrors of rock-crystal and crystalline glass, and her palaces contained a number of Venetian mirrors. In seventeenth-century England (as in France and the Low Countries) borders were simple, of receding section, with moulding made of ebony, olive, walnut, or Grenoble wood. The outer shape of these mirrors was either octagonal or rectangular, with fretted pediment. The 'fruit and flowers' style of the beginning of the century was executed both in marquetry and in *ronde-bosse* carving. Many dressing-table mirrors of the period were in stumpwork (Ill. 172). In the inventory of Charles I a mirror in ebony, amber, mother-of-pearl, shell and embroidery is listed.

In the middle of the seventeenth century, the manner of Louis XIV's court is adopted: borders are covered at corners and centres with ornaments of repoussé, gilded or silvered copper. The Royal Collection at Windsor contains two of these mirrors with the arms of Charles II and William III.

At the beginning of the reign of Charles II, the monumental carver Grinling Gibbons (1648–1720) created a new style. His frames were of cedar or pine enriched with a studied disorder of fruit, flowers, cherubim and draperies, treated with such naturalism that a much-impressed contemporary pointed out that 'every leaf is like to tremble at the passing of a carriage'. A pair of chequered mirrors (in Queen Mary's Gallery, Kensington Palace) attributed to Grinling Gibbons, are bordered with draperies, trophies, palms, trumpets and garlands of flowers. At the close of the century, many mirror-frames were decorated with Bantamwork (lacquer), using panels imported from China and Japan.

V.   Mirror frame. Paintings in verre églomisé. Flanders. 17th c.

VI.   Sumptuous Baroque frame. Italy? 17th c.

VII.   Mirror with pediment. Frame in blue
crystal glass. By Precht. Sweden. 18th c.

VIII.   Hall of mirrors in Linderhof Castle.
Bavaria. 1870–74.

At the beginning of the eighteenth century, under the influence of Daniel Marot, carved gilt frames were used, with fretted and pierced pediments. Some fine examples are to be found in the dining-room at Hampton Court and in the Victoria and Albert Museum. At the same period there began to be a great call for *verre églomisé* (unfired colours and gilding applied to the back of the glass and protected by varnish or another sheet of glass) in red, green, or black, decorated with gilt arabesques. A mirror of this type, with the arms of the Earl of Leicester, is to be found at Penshurst Place; in William III's room at Hampton Court, there is a mirror surrounded by a border in blue glass, with crown and cypher of the King cresting the pediment. As in France, overmantel mirrors and pier-glasses often had an oil painting forming the upper portion (several examples are on view at Hampton Court). Under the reign of George I, a new type of mirror frame appeared, in carved gilt wood in fretted form, often with candle brackets, the framing being of walnut or mahogany decorated with gesso (see Ill. 182–185). The one surmounted by feathers, at Hampton Court, was made for Frederick, Prince of Wales. Some frames of the same period are also architectural, comprising architrave and base, and harmonizing with the interior architecture designed by contemporary architects such as Colin Campbell, Gibbs and Ripley. In the middle of the century, the Chippendale style held sway, with ist Chinese influence: pagodas, waterfalls, coquillages and birds were the most frequent motifs. (See also Ill. 191.) Matthias Lock and Thomas Johnson were also good mirror designers in the same style (examples in St. Giles's House, Dorset, and Victoria and Albert Museum). During this period, as in France, toilet-cases and dance cards were magnificent articles of rococo jewellery, made in gold, bloodstone, agate and ribbon agate.

Towards the close of the century, 'sun-mirrors' appear, sometimes with a head of Apollo, in carved wood, in the centre of the mirror. After 1765, the rococo style was ousted by that of Adam; the classical revival brought back ornamentation in the form of sphinxes, urns and medallions.

Throughout the whole of the eighteenth century one finds the psyche, or swing-mirror, usually in lacquer; towards the close of the century it lost its drawers and became larger, taking then the name of cheval-glass or horse dressing-table. The use of the word 'horse' is explained in an English dictionary by the four feet of the mirror; an American dictionary prefers the view that the mirror was large enough for a horse to see himself in it!

(e) *Spain*. Spain openly encouraged foreign masters and artistic trends. The great influence of the Italian Renaissance is to be seen in Spanish architectural, polychrome frames, frames with Greek corners or in silvered gesso; and her debt to the Low Countries is shown by the use of simple receding mouldings of ebony, or overlaid with shell. From this period date the large mirrors kept at the Convent of Guadalupe and the Escurial; their frames are in the style of Venetian octagonal mirrors, with recessed and receding section. The ornate mirrors we reproduce in ill. 249–252 are among the most lavish ever created. The octagonal mirror in ill. 254, so reminiscent of the Louis XIII style, has mouldings of carved gilt wood adorned with fruit and foliage; the glass compartements are decorated realistically with painted flowers (particularly tulips, which are also to be found painted on glass mirror borders in the drawing-room at the Convent of Guadalupe). We have discerned a Moorish influence in certain frames decorated with small pieces of glass held by cemented hemp (Ill. 256), and also in iron openwork frames.

The national character expresses itself in frames with strongly marked carving whose ornamentation represents a clasp and strap motif; gilding is thick, and polychrome rich. As forms became more varied, they led gradually to the Churrigueresque style, which is merely a pretext for ornamental divagation. French influence is to be seen at the close of the eighteenth century, in mirrors plated with silver and gold. The 'Germains' were commissioned in 1756 to make the silver-gilt toilet-case intended for the Princess of Asturias.

Mirrors are more particularly to be found in churches and convents — for example, in the sacristy of the Escurial, in the cathedrals of Segovia and Valladolid, in San Francesco church, Avila, in the chapel of the Convent of Guadalupe, in San Juan de Dios and San Justo, Grenada, and in the sacristy of Salamanca cathedral.

(f) *Portugal*. We would draw attention to the small dressing-cases reproduced in ill. 260. At the 'Trésors de l'Orfèvrerie du Portugal' exhibition in 1955, item No. 168 was a travelling toilet-set in silver-gilt consisting of thirty-one pieces, one of them a mirror of Peter II (1683–1706) style, in a wooden box lined with green velvet (kept at the Arte Antiga Museum, Lisbon). Item No. 446 was a toilet-service in silver-gilt made by 'F. T. Germain, carver and silversmith to the King at the Galleries of the Louvre in Paris' in 1765; the mirror bears the date 1766, and is probably the one mentioned in inventories: 'F. T. Germain makes in 1766 a mirror for the Princess of Portugal, surmounted by a Cupid about to crown Beauty' (reproduced in H. Bouilhet, *Orfèvrerie française*, p. 169). The French architect Meissonier designed for Portugal a room decorated with mirrors.

(g) *Flanders and the Low Countries.* In the Middle Ages, the reputation of Flemish mirrors in crystalline glass spread far and wide. In fact, the Venetians set up a mirror factory in Murano in imitation of the Flemish ones. Flemish and Dutch ornamentalists created styles particular to their countries. Johannes Fredeman de Vriese, the famous sixteenth century architect, designed a mirror-frame with ornamentation of carved strapwork, together with a mixture of animals, birds, flowers and fruit, all bound by ribbons and draperies. An etching by Crispin the Elder (1536–1601) shows a frame adorned with strapwork, heads and sphinxes. The palace of Amerungen contains a curious frame of carved gilt wood bordered with a wide ribbon hung with heavy foliage. In the early seventeenth century, as a reaction against the Renaissance, mirror-frames were, just as in England and France, simple borders of black wood, guilloched or overlaid with shell. In mid-century, Jan Lutma (1609–1689) created the so-called 'auricular' style, which has a cartilaginous appearance; this enjoyed great success in decorative carving and in gold and silver work, also achieving popularity in Germany. Gerbrandt van den Eeckhout, who worked during this period, made drawings for frames in the same style, with undulations and coquillages, and this style is to be found in the mirror-frames adorning the dollshouses at the Zentral Museum, Utrecht. The Nederlandisches Museum, Amsterdam, has an auricular frame decorated with trophies, and a cavalier on the pediment. At the Rijksmuseum in Amsterdam there is a mirror-frame with a flat ground upon which is carved a meticulous arrangement of toilet articles (Ill. 110).

At the S. R. exhibition of 1934, item No. 21 was a mirror with support in a silver-gilt frame, hall-marked 'The Hague 1680', and bearing the arms of the Ilchester family; it was part of a dressing-case (J. Helft collection). No. 22 at the same exhibition was a mirror with support in a frame of black and gold lacquer, adorned with palmettes on the pediment (P. Callieux collection). A toilet-case with mirror in silver-gilt dated 1675 was seen at the 'Chefs-d'oeuvre de la curiosité du monde' exhibition in 1954. It came from the Premsela and Hamburger collection in Amsterdam. (See also ill. 114).

At the close of the seventeenth century, Holland underwent the influence of the Frenchman Daniel Marot (1650–1718), who became the Prince of Orange's architect in 1685. His engravings appeared in Amsterdam in 1712 and had enormous success. This influence is revealed in many French-style overmantel mirrors in private houses at The Hague and in the State Museum in Amsterdam, in mirror-frames with canopies, and in mirrors with gold and silver work.

Antwerp was the foremost market for articles imported from China during the whole of the eighteenth century. The abundance of lacquers, in particular, led to the creation of large numbers of frames in Chinese or 'Chinese-style' lacquer.

In 1760 appeared G. de Grendel's new book on chimney-pieces. Mirror-plate was often used at this period to help in the lighting of rooms. At the end of the century, a Flemish edition of the iconology of Jean-Charles Delafosse, spread the ornamental repertoire of the Louis XVI period throughout the Low countries.

(*b*) *Italy*. The greater part of Italian mirrors were produced in Venice. At least six different types were created there during the seventeenth and eighteenth centuries. The architectural mirrors of the sixteenth century continued to be made at the beginning of the seventeenth (walnut mirror in the Correr Museum, another of triangular shape in the former Bonafé collection). At the close of the century, one finds a type of mirror with pediment and border of cut glass, usually blue; the one in Ill. 214 is in Mr. Devinoy's collection.

In the eighteenth century, the silvered mirror was engraved and set in mouldings enriched with carved gilt wood (Palazzo Rezzonico; Villa Lazzara Pisani in Stra; Serge Roche and J. Rotil collection). Carved gilt wood tended to disappear at the close of the century, in favour of borders of engraved glass, adorned with glass thread and glass flowers. The overmantel mirror, contrary to the French type, was of very elongated proportions, cut into three parts vertically (Ill. 222). Mirror-plates used in the ligthing of palaces were often engraved and framed with carved gilt wood, glass, thread, Bassano or Capo die Monte faience (see Ill. 230).

The last type of eighteenth-century Venetian mirror was the lacquer variety, often found in dressing-table mirrors. The gilt decoration was put on a ground of black, green, blue or red lacquer (Ill. 234).

A Frenchman travelling in Italy in 1765 described the royal palace at Turin thus: 'The furnishings harmonize with the beauty of the rooms: among other things to be seen there are candle brackets of which the plaques are mirrors set in heavy silver frames wrought most tastefully. We remark upon them only because this particular kind of furniture is much used in Italian rooms, usually distributed round the sides so as to throw more light therein'.

A convex mirror surrounded with crystal, pearls and gold, is to be seen at the palace of Isola Bella. The royal palace of Genoa possesses several large mirrors with pediments of carved gilt wood with decorations in the style of Bérain, on a ground of red glass. A Genoese mirror with ornate periphery of trophies, arms and coquillages on carved gilt wood is reproduced in ill. 218.

Naples made more use of borders of coral — a substance which, so the saying goes, was 'formed with the blood of Medusa'. Bronze and coral are used in the frame shown in ill. 211. Sometimes mother-of-pearl is used

Leaf of door in gilt wood and mirror glass. Genoa. Early 18th c. Amid the vines and foliage cupids, sirens, dragons, grotesques and cornucopia are to be seen. 2.75 × 1.28 m. Serge Roche & Rotil.

with coral (San Martino, Naples). In the S. R. exhibition, 1934, there was a double-sided mirror in bronze and jasper made in the seventeenth century (Landau collection).

A few ornamentalists concerned themselves with the problem of mirror-frames: Frederico Zuccano (1536–1602) designed borders enriched with female head-and-shoulder figurines and garlands of fruit. In Rome, during the first half of the seventeenth century, Bernadus Castellux made designs for mirrors decorated with winged busts, amorini, and garlands of fruit. In 1753, Angelo Rossi, of Florence, decorated an overmantel mirror with draperies, figures, arms and scrolls.

Mirror with pediment in red lacquered wood, bronze and precious stones. Late 16th c. 0.48 × 0.56 m. Pierre Delbée Collection.

CHAPTER FOUR

Mirror Galleries and Mirror Rooms

From time immemorial, Man has sought his image in mirrors; from the beginning of the seventeenth century, he adapted the larger mirrors then available for decorative use. But it was only in the mideighteenth century that it occurred to him to use mirrors to double the size of rooms, and to increase the brilliance of light coming from wall-brackets and chandeliers. This new material, mirror plate, was set in panelling or in decorative gesso frames, and in the eighteenth century, even ceilings were decorated with mirrors. Large mirror plate was used in 'galleries', long rooms used for balls and banquets, and in *cabinets*, small rooms set aside for conversation or study.

Mirror Galleries

The most famous example is the hall or mirrors at the palace of Versailles. It has seventeen arched doors, adorned with bevelled mirrors in bronze gilt mouldings, stretching rhythmically for two hundred and twenty-five feet, and harmonizing with the windows. Jules Hardouin Mansart erected this gallery in 1679 on the terrace built by Le Vau, 'a gigantic balcony from which the King and his Court could watch the sunlight playing on the fountains, amid a setting of trees and flowers'. The gallery of the *Roi Soleil* truly created the style used for those subsequently built all over Europe. Here are some of the most important:

The gallery of the Hôtel de La Vrillière, in Paris, by Robert de Cotte.

The Gallery of Charles XI at the palace of Stockholm *c.* 1690.

The great gallery of the palace of Schönbrunn, by Nicolas Pacassi, and that of Hetzendorf palace (both near Vienna).

The great gilt gallery of the palace of Charlottenburg, by Georg Wenzeslaus von Knobelsdorff, in very ornate rococo style.

The great gallery of the Residence at Stuttgart, built in 1753 and reminiscent of the Louis XIV style. The banqueting-hall at Augsburg (Schaezlerhaus), in rococo style with three horizontal rows of candle brackets.

Louis II of Bavaria had a copy of the hall of mirrors at Versailles built (1870–1880) in his palace at Herrenchiemsee. He also found in the mirror rooms of his palace at Linderhof (decorated in 1878 by Joseph de la Paix) an incentive to self-contemplation and escapism.

In the present Chamber of Commerce of Genoa there is a gallery decorated with doors of mirror-plate and carved gilt wood, of which there are two examples in the Serge Roche and J. Rotil collection (see ill. on page 32).

Mirror Rooms

France — The mirror room of Catherine de Medici (1599) contained 'one hundred and nineteen Venice mirrors set in the panelling'. That of Mlle de La Vallière (1668) comprised one hundred and forty-four mirrors. With the seventeenth century *Précieuses*, the mirror room became indispensable. Among the most famous are those of La Grande Mademoiselle at Saint-Fargeau and at the Luxembourg ('I fitted out my room with many paintings and mirrors, I was enchanted and thought I had made the most beautiful thing in the world'), and that of the Duchess of Bouillon decorated by Audran. At Versailles, the Council Chamber was lined with mirrors, and on small console tables of carved gilt wood were arranged magnificent objects in rock-crystal (these are now in the Galerie d'Apollon, at the Louvre).

At the home of Mazarin, the mirrors were mainly Venetian, and at the château of Vaux-le-Vicomte (built by Le Vau for Fouquet) there was a much admired room, painted, panelled and 'embellished with mirrors'. The Dauphin's room at Versailles is described by Félibien as having 'round the sides and on the ceiling mirrors with compartments and borders gilded upon a ground of ebony marquetry'. In the mirror room of the Hôtel de Lorge, famous for its view, one could see 'the hill of Montmartre, the plain of Saint-Denis and the village of Porcherons reflected in a series of mirrors'. The mirror room of the château of Maisons-Laffitte has just been restored by the architect J.-Ch. Moreux. The *Régent* was not content with having a mirror room; he lined the walls of his own room with mirrors. Marie-Antoinette's bathroom at Trianon was decorated entirely with mirrors embellished with fine paintings and framed with arabesques (these mirrors now adorn the Emperor's room at the château of Fontainebleau).

At Bagatelle, the boudoir was garnished with mirrors 'which reflected from all sides the positions of the lovers'.

Under the First Empire, the bathroom of the Hôtel de Beauharnais was decorated in Pompeian style. Slender colonettes painted like marble were reflected to infinity in the walls of mirror (Ill. 108). The Second Empire bathroom of Eugénie de Montijo at the Palais de l'Elysée is remarkable. Percier and Fontaine designed vistas of mirrors at the Palais des Tuileries. The boudoir of Mlle d'Hervieu had the walls, ceiling and floor lined with mirrors without a single space in between them (Caillot).

Holland — The idea of mirror rooms adorned with Chinese porcelain and Delft-ware probably originated in the Low Countries, which had established connections with the countries of the Far East very early on. The Swedish architect, Nicodemus Tessin, returning from Holland in 1687, described the audience chamber of the Princess of Orange at her country house in Unsslardiek, near The Hague, noting veneers of imported Chinese lacquer, a mirror-lined ceiling, and an abundance of china-ware decorating particularly the overmantel mirror.

Germany — Mirror rooms attained their greatest popularity in Germany, especially in the baroque and rococo Bavarian châteaux of the eighteenth century. The carved gilt panelling bordering the mirrors is usually graced with numerous console tables bearing collections of Delft-ware, Chinese and Japanese porcelain, and later, Dresden and Strasbourg china. In the second half of the eighteenth century, the popularity of these collections of ceramics tended to disappear, and mirror decoration usually took the form of paintings in Chinese style.

At the palace of Charlottenburg, built in 1706 by Eosander von Göthe, the walls (including the cornices) are covered with Chinese porcelain plates and vases which stand out from the background of mirror plate. At the palace of Gaibach, built 1709–1713 by Lohr, the panels of mirror are graced by numerous small Chinese *magots*. At the palace of Pommersfelden, built 1714–1719 by Ferdinand Plitzner, a collection of Chinese vases and *magots* is distributed over the walnut and carved gilt panelling, and over the mirrors. The blue ceiling is embellished with mirrors and white stucco (Ill. 135).

One of the most characteristic summer residences of the eighteenth century is La Favorite (architecture by Rossi and Röhrer, decoration by by Pfleger and H. G. Stöhr), built near Rastatt for Ludwig-Wilhelm, Margrave of Baden, godson of Louis XIV. The mirror room preceding the bedroom contains a collection of china from the factory of Hannong at Strasbourg. Mirrors are set into the window-embrasures. In the 'Florentine' room (a counterpart of the mirror room) the walls are decorated with panels of lacquer, mosaic, marble, alabaster, mother-of-pearl and hard stones; and in the squares of the leaded mirror glass are medaillons painted on ivory representing the greatest philosophers, scholars and artists of all times (Ill. 146 and 147).

At the palace of Ludwigsburg, built by Johann Friedrich Nette in 1716, the walls and ceilings are lined with mirrors of round, oval and irregularly curved outline. Antonio Bossi's stucco ceilings are studded with spherical mirrors to increase the intensity of the light from the chandeliers. At the palace of Weikersheim built in 1717 by Vogt von Oehringen, a collection of Chinese porcelain statuettes is placed on hundreds of gilt console tables. In 1720, the architect J. M. Hoppenhaupt eliminated the porcelain element from the decoration of the mirror room at the palace of Merseburg, so as to show off the mirrors and gilt wood to all their advantage. The ceiling is a superb example of perspective in mirror plate. The same architect was responsible for Frederick the Great's study in his palace in Berlin; there, the chequered mirrors alternate with palms. G. Hennicke decorated a ceiling of the palace of Wiesentheid with mirrors and stucco. The Munich Residence (destroyed during the last war) contained an ornament room and a mirror room decorated after a design by the French architect François Cuvilliés between 1731 and 1733 (carved panelling by J. Dietrich and W. Miroffsky). The same architect (stucco work by J. B. Zimmermann) designed in 1739 an ostentatious arrangement of large mirrors in silver-plated frames on a blue wall, in the residence at Amalienburg, in Nymphenburg park (Ills. 148, 149 and 151).

See also illustrations and notes for Ansbach (159 and 160), Würzburg (154), Bayreuth (163 and 164). The Munich Residence also contained a mirror drawing-room in Louis XVI style designed by the French architect C.-P. Puille in 1799 (carved panelling by P. P. Schöpf). Mirrors are used to decorate the window-embrasures at the little palace of Schönbusch, near Aschaffenburg (c. 1780) and in the red room at Berlin Palace. French mirror-makers (e.g. Grainer, in 1731) supplied mirrors for many Bavarian residences.

England — At Buckingham Palace, an eighteenth-century music room is decorated with doors and niches of mirror glass. At Syon House (Middlesex) there is a room in which mirrors alternate with Chinese wallpaper. Northumberland House had a mirror room designed by Adam[1];

[1] Now in the Victoria and Albert Museum.

and during the Regency period, Nash decorated a drawing-room of Brighton Pavilion, of which the mirror-lined walls and the doors are embellished with panels of appliqué carved wood.[2]

Austria — At the close of the eighteenth century, Daniel Gran decorated the 'gilded room' of the Albertina in Vienna; flowers are painted on a gold background, the mantelpiece is in lapis-lazuli, the overmantel, alcoves and doors of mirror.

Italy — Architects constructed mirror rooms without resorting to the use of ceramics, depending entirely on carved gilt wood for decorating the mirrors — in contrast to most German residences. The Palazzo Terzi at Bergamo is one of the most perfect examples of this mirror and gilt wood type of architecture. The chapel of Borromeo Palace is decorated in the same style, but is further embellished with engraved mirrors. The Queen's room in Turin is decorated with mirrors. At the Palazzo Isnardi (Castello), now an academy of music, there is an octagonal mirror drawing-room by Alfieri (stucco work by Ladatte and Bolfieri). This room probably served as a model for the fantastic *salon* of the Grévin museum. Rooms of the royal castle of Stupinigi are described in notes to ill. 246. The Palazzo Litta (Milan) contains large mirrors with broken pediments (Ill. 248). The ducal palace of Mantua has a 'galleria degli specchi' in eighteenth-century neo-classical style. The ball-room of the Palazzo Riccardi, in Florence, is decorated with painted mirrors. The royal palace of Genoa has pilasters of mirror glass. In Venice, at the Palazzo Rezzonico, there are doors of mirror plate with painted panels. Mirror plate is used at Bagheria and in the chapel of the royal palace at Palermo. At Palagonia, there is a ceiling of mirrors embellished with blue and white painted stucco. For the Italian Embassy in Paris, the decorateur Lœwi created a theatre with a stage incorporating mirrors arranged in perspective. Large panels of mirror plate and carved gilt wood (taken from a palace in Palermo), alternating with large polychrome panels, decorate the same room. At the Musée des Arts Décoratifs one can see mirrors set in panels, removed from a palace in Palermo. The bedroom of Countess Jean de Polignac, in Paris, has a panelled decoration from a Venetian palace; only the pilasters, cornice and base, enriched with mirrors, have been preserved.

[2] In a letter (in French) to Mme de Monconseil, Lord Chesterfield described his 'boudoir' at Chesterfield House, South Audley Street, built by Isaac Ware: '…above the mantelpiece, which is by Giallo di Sienna, are many mirrors, carvings, and much gilt, and in the centre the portrait of a very lovely woman by La Rosalba.' 5 Sept. 1748 (ed. Bonamy Dobrée, Vol. iv).

Spain — The sanctuary of the Convent of Guadalupe is adorned with mirrors on which birds, tulips and angels' heads have been painted (Ill. 253). Mirrors are also used in the chapel at Paular, in a drawing-room of the royal palace at Madrid, and in the sacristy of the Escorial. In the billiard-room at Aranjuez, the overmantels and trumeaux are decorated with mirrors *églomisé* black and gold.

Portugal — The royal palace at Queluz was built by Mateo Vicente (1710–1786) with J.-B. Robillon collaborating for the decoration and garden lay-out. This is one of the finest examples in the whole of Europe of the use of mirrors. In each room of the palace the arrangement of painted wall-space and mirror panelling is different. In the throne room, the architect used mirror plate for the polygonal columns, the oval mirrors adorning the walls, the great pilasters between the windows; and also in the depth of the wall above the doors, made into niches graced by vases which are reflected in mirrors. In the Ambassador's room, the doors and pilasters are adorned with mirrors. In the Queen's room the mirror decoration is reserved for the doors and the square columns supporting the cupola. The Queen's boudoir, a small room in French rococo style, is decorated with chequered mirrors, the joins between them being concealed by carved gilt wood. In the centre of each square is a painting on glass in a rococo frame. In another room the octagonal overdoors alone are decorated with mirrors (Ill. 266).

Russia — In her palace of Tsarkoye Selo, Catherine II had the English architect Cameron to decorate a bedroom with mirrors, faience, glass and bronze, and a smoking-room with mirrors and with glass backed with coloured flannel.

Sweden — In the pavilion of Gustav III at Haga, the walls of mirrors, bordered with pilasters of gilt and painted carved wood, reflect the park of the château.

CHAPTER FIVE
Far East, Middle East, Near East, Africa, America

During and after the Middle Ages, China continued her traditional production of bronze mirrors. A painting on silk of the fourth century, attributed to Ku K'ai Chih (British Museum), shows a bronze mirror attached to a pedestal. In a painting by Su Han-ch'en (*c.* 1115–1170) (Museum of Fine Art, Boston), we see a lady looking at herself in a large circular mirror.

In the seventeenth and eighteenth centuries, the borders of silvered mirrors were lacquered or decorated with champlevé enamel. In China during the seventeenth century there appeared curious paintings whose chaotic outlines become meaningful only when reflected in a cylinder or cone of silvered glass, which is placed at the centre of the painting. These catoptrical anamorphoses originated in the European anamorphoses of the sixteenth century, which consist of paintings one has to view obliquely, without the use of a cylindrical mirror. These paintings, both Oriental and European, merely apply the optical theories which were enunciated by the mathematicians of antiquity, and utilized by the magicians of the Middle Ages. We reproduce one of these Chinese paintings in ill. 34, and have noticed several European catoptrical anamorphoses in the collections of Jacques Dupont and Charles Ratton.

Japan has left us the marvellous legend of Matsuyama Kagani, in which the metal mirror plays a magical rôle. In many Japanese prints (by Susuki Harunobu, Outamaro, etc.) courtesans are shown peering into lacquered mirrors.

The ancient tradition of the round bronze mirror continued in Egypt. At the exhibition of Byzantine art (Musée des Arts Décoratifs, 1931) there was a mirror-case of engraved ivory representing a seated woman holding a mirror in her left hand (Alexandria, third century). (See also ills. 22 and 24).

Persian mirrors were influenced by China and Egypt. In the Landau collection are two round bronze mirrors (thirteenth century) found during excavations at Hamadan. (See also ills. 27 and 28). In Persia, during the nineteenth century, there were many specimens found of silvered mirrors contained in small cupboards with two shutters having polychrome floral

Le Bon Genre, N.º 29.

IX. "Le Lever des Grisettes". Colored copperplate print. France. About 1805.

X. Mirror with frame in gilt wood and Bohemian glass. Germany. Early 17th c.

XI. Overmantel mirror frame in gilt wood. France. End of 18th c.

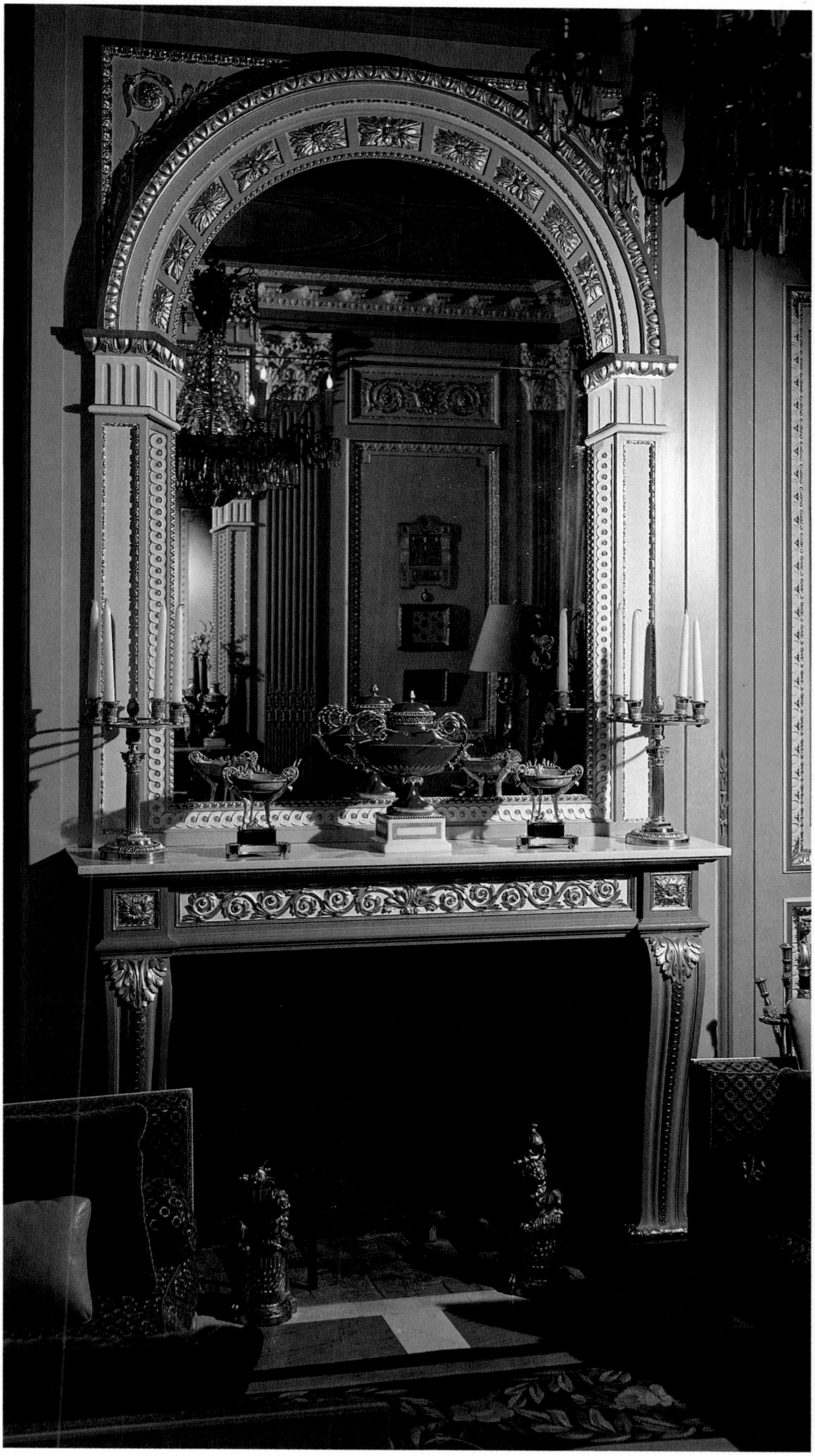

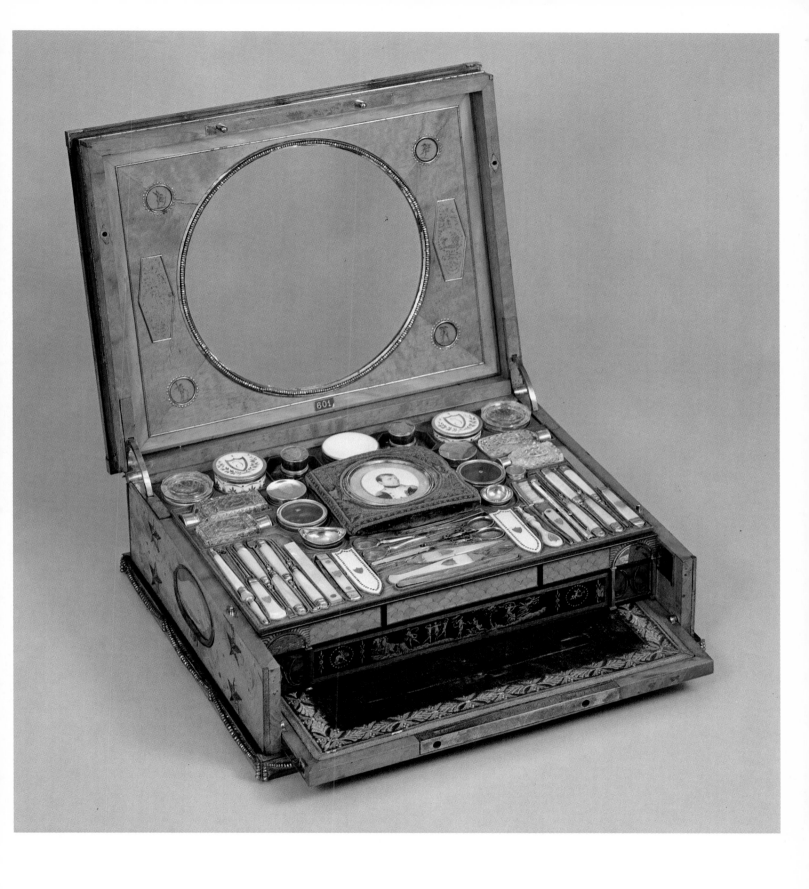

XII.   Vanity-case of Empress Josephine. By Félix Remond. France. About 1805.

decoration. The Persians were large importers of Venetian mirrors, which are still to be seen in large numbers in palaces there.

Several Turkish mirrors figured in the 'Splendours of Turkish Art' exhibition (Museé des Arts Décoratifs, 1953). Item No. 188 was a mirror in carved ivory of oval shape, adorned with Seljukian motifs, the mount bearing the names of Solyman the Magnificent and the sculptor Gani, and the date 1543 (Topkapi Sarayi Museum). No. 189 was a similar mirror, but round and incrusted with turquoises (Topkapi Sarayi Museum), and Nos. 177–182 consisted of several nineteenth-century mirrors in silver and silver-gilt from the Pozzi and Grédy collections.

In America, mirrors of obsidian (natural volcanic glass), iron pyrites and copper, dating from the pre-Columbian period have been found (see ill. 33).

Use of Mirrors for Light Effects — Very small pieces of silvered glass have long been used to produce a variety of sparkling effects. The technique (which offered a use for broken mirror glass) seems to have originated in the East, and was spread throughout the Mediterranean basin by the Moorish conquerors. One finds it used in Spain, in mirror frames covered with fragments of mirror set in cemented hemp (Ill. 256); often, the clothing of the Saints for feast days and processions has small mirrors set among the embroidery.

In Sicily, harnesses are often decorated with these small pieces of mirror set in metal, and extraordinary parasols are to be seen there, adorned with constellations of small mirrors.

Turkish and Persian palaces were decorated with small fragments of mirror stuck on to fresh plaster. The most famous examples are those of the Golestan Palace in Teheran, and a palace in Schiraz, in which walls and vaulted ceilings are covered entirely with these reflecting facets which produce the most extraordinary light effects imaginable. If a light is placed in the centre of the room, it is multiplied so much that one has the impression of a starry sky.

In India and in Siam, small mirrors are used to adorn head-dresses and certain articles of apparel. In Africa, small pieces of mirror are affixed to Gaboon-masks and to 'Nduda' reliquary statues from Zaire containing charms (Ill. 20). In Guinea, dancers' head-dresses are adorned with many small fragments of mirror.

In our own part of the world, this technique of reflected scintillation came to an inglorious end, in the nineteenth century, on merry-go-rounds and fair-booths. One could compare the rococo ornamentation which accompanies these small mirrors, with some of the decorations in Bavarian and Austrian churches.

CHAPTER SIX

The Nineteenth Century

The use of mirrors went on developing throughout the nineteenth century, thanks to new technical inventions; but the mirror proper, as an article, lost much of its quality and entered a period of veritable decadence at the close of the century. The English cheval-glass was adapted to French neo-classicism, and resulted in the 'psyche' during the Empire period. Percier designed the 'psyche toilet-set', made by Jacob for the Empress Josephine (Musée des Arts Décoratifs). G. Jacob was the designer of a small dressing-table of mahogany, ebony and copper strips, for use placed on the knees. It is in Mme H. Lefuel's collection. The Empress Josephine ordered from Biennais a small psyche in gnarled ash, with strips of ebony and bronze gilt (in the same collection). The Malmaison museum has a dressing-table in bird's-eye mahogany and bronze gilt, also by Biennais. The dressing-table designed by N.-H. Jacob for the Empress Marie-Louise (Grognot and Joinel collection) is in Vonèche crystal and bronze gilt, and contains a little mechanical organ which plays a selection of thirteen tunes. Biennais made the famous toilet-case of Jérôme Bonaparte, of ebony enriched with plaques of *verre églomisé* on an aventurine ground (M. Geffroy collection). The same silversmith made Josephine's hand-mirror, bearing the arms of Napoleon and Josephine (former Bernard Franck collection). In the Hermès collection we have noticed several nineteenth century toilet-cases with fine silverplated mirrors: one silver toilet-case mirror which belonged to Dr Antommarchi, who went with Napoleon to Saint Helena; the toilet-case in silver-gilt belonging to Queen Maria-Amelia, and the Prince Imperial's travelling toilet-case in silver, both by Aucoc the elder (see also ill. 102). The Empire period also produced overmantel mirrors and pier-glasses framed with mahogany and enriched with bronze, the pediment being supported by caryatids.

At the beinning of the century, many curved mirrors in Sheraton style were produced, with frames of carved gilt wood, and highly carved pediments often crested with an eagle (Victoria and Albert Museum). (See ills 201 and 202; and ill. 128 for a curious Swiss 'mechanical' hand-mirror).

In the Musée des Arts Décoratifs there is a large musical psyche (once belonging to the Duchess of Angoulême), dating from the French Restoration period. Many mirrors of this period have borders of *verre églomisé*, usually on a white ground, with gilt decorations. (See also ill. 98.) A round mirror supported by a bronze Cupid resting on a cylindrical foot of cut crystal is kept in the Serge Roche collection.

During the romantic period, mirrors in 'troubadour' style, with bronze imitation Gothic frames were popular (Ill. 102).

Throughout the nineteenth century, until our own day, Venice continued and continues to produce its traditional type of mirror, enriched with spun glass mouldings and glass flowers, usually polychrome.

In 1857, the Frenchman François Petit-Jean made practicable the method invented by Liebig for tinning glass with silver, in place of the mercury which had been used since the sixteenth century. This new technique gave clearer mirrors, and had no bad effects on the worker's health; it was imported into England under the reign of Queen Victoria, and then spread throughout Europe. Also during this period, the Dodé method of platizining glass began to be used; this transforms the glass into a mirror only if it is lit from in front — if the light comes from behind, it no longer reflects. In 1860 there were six glasshouses in England, five in France, two in Germany, one in Italy, and two in Belgium.

Under Louis-Philippe, the psyche was dethroned by the mirror-wardrobe. Here are two very contrary views about this new article of furniture. Théodore de Banville wrote: 'A monster has invented, made, and distributed over the face of the earth, the most hideously mediocre, the most vulgarly stupid, the most unspeakably crude of all furniture: the mirror-wardrobe. O God! despite the wealth of tortures of all kinds handed down to us from the Middle Ages, not one of these tortures has been applied to the guilty perpetrator.' But Barbey d'Aurevilly said: 'I confess I have a weakness for this ugly thing, the mirror-wardrobe. To me, it is not a piece of furniture, but a great lake in which I see my ideas floating, together with my reflection.' What, then, are we to think of the famous dressing-room of Mme Ellini, 'hung with violet satin and adorned with mirror-wardrobes and psyches'!

During the reign of Napoleon III, the art of pastiche (or of plagiarism, as Guillaume Janneau prefers to call it) was perfected. The gilt composition frame ruled supreme, and its unfortunate popularity continued until the close of the century. The hand-mirror regained favour at this period; a silver one by Perreux can be seen at the Musée des Arts Décoratifs. At the turn of the century, the 'Fabergé' (Russian jewellers to royalty) made toilet-cases with mirrors, as well as their famous 'mechanical' pieces. Baccarat created several mirrors with borders of cut glass in imitation of the early Venetian style.

The romatic story of the mirror seems to end in the worst possible taste; and at the same time, paradoxically, mirror plate was put to more and more uses, in blocks of flats, cafés, confectioners and butchers' shops. Even furniture was made of mirror plate — for example, the seat (part of a suite) which was shown at the S. R. exhibition in 1934 (item No. 90); it was made by Baccarat about 1860 for sultan Abd-ul-Hamid, and was completely overlaid with engraved mirrors. Public buildings were also decorated with mirrors: the Hôtel de Ville in Paris, the Casino in Monaco, the Hôtel Continental, and the Paris Opéra were all fitted with very large mirrors from the glass-works at Saint-Gobain.

Art Nouveau and Art Deco

ART NOUVEAU

In the second half of the nineteenth century interior decoration was characterized by its use of rigid forms and its insistence for reasons of historical versimilitude on often contradictory forms of ornamentation. This eclectic coexistence of styles from different epochs prevented the emergence of a new homogeneity. Architecture and interior decoration were dominated by artificial pomp and increasingly industrial means of reproduction. Desire for a radical renewal within the arts and crafts often went hand in hand with ideas on social reform which regarded industrialization as the cause for the decline of the arts. As early as 1857 William Morris and Arthur Mackmurdo began attacking the new age of industrialization and demanding a return to the medieval guild system (hence the name 'Century Guild' for their movement) and to an exclusively handcrafted production of goods. They advocated a revitalization of the whole of art on the basis of maximum simplicity and relevant functionalism.

The Glasgow School, which was founded by Charles Rennie Mackintosh, borrowed heavily from the Pre-Raphaelites and Japanese art, and its delicate lines created basic cubic forms in exquisite rhythm. The Willow Tea Rooms, designed by Mackintosh in 1904, are completely panelled with wall mirrors which themselves are enlivened by the delicate ornamental effect of sections of coloured glass in Oriental style. In accordance with the new theory the mirrors formed a unity with the interior as a whole.

The American, Louis Comfort Tiffany, concerned himself with various aspects of the decorative arts and was likewise inspired by Japanese models as well as by Classical antiquity. He studied the technique of glass production and succeeded in opalizing antique glass synthetically. His choice of ornamentation is characterized by butterflies, delicate flowers, pearl oysters and other such fragile, iridiscent forms. In the Museum of Modern Art in New York there is a hand mirror influenced by Tiffany in the stylized form of a peacock. The bird's arched neck forms the handle while the feathers are in enamel with inlaid sapphires (Ill. 271).

This rejection of historical styles and the quest for a synthesis of the arts encompassing all spheres of life very soon also became a conspicuous feature of Viennese art circles. During the last decades of the nineteenth century the reform program of the Austrian Museum für Kunst und Industrie (founded in 1864) rejecting historical versimilitude in art largely reflected the tastes of the prosperous middle classes in architecture and furniture design.

It was not, however, until the founding of the artists' community Sezession, that the new ideas concerning the equal status of the applied arts began gaining ground. At the 1900 World Exhibition Josef Hoffmann and Joseph Maria Olbrich demonstrated the new Viennese style in a very convincing manner. Under the influence of English artists such as Charles Robert Ashbee and Charles Rennie Mackintosh and of the German Biedermeier tradition this style aimed at achieving maximum unity, a clear conception of furniture form, and a decorative idiom based principally on plant motifs, which in the case of Josef Hoffmann was invariably highly stylized. Rare types of wood were left untreated whilst others were stained blue, green, red and violet. Since articles of furniture were regarded as works of art great importance was attached to ornamentation. Marquetry, carving, coloured glass, and exquisite materials such as ivory, mother-of-pearl, tortoiseshell, and marble were all used. A dressing table by Franz Messner (1900) in grey maple wood is designed along the lines of the basic forms of rectangle and square. The mirror is mounted between two flanking cabinet sections and the table with drawers rests on a right-angled slatted stand. The copper mountings and brass mirror frame together with the bevelled glass give the dressing table all the qualities of an exquisite piece of cabinetwork (Ill. 288). The mirror frame by the woodcarver Franz Viehweider (1901) is made of untreated pearwood and is shaped in the form of stylized foliage with naturalistic cherry flowers in pale hues as a contrast (Ill. 292). This floral mirror can be compared with a much more austere frame by Sigmund Jaray (Ill. 291) in which the wood's natural grain stands out in lively contrast to the frame's extremely scanty ornamentation consisting solely of vertical grooves and circles.

After Olbrich's appointment by Archduke Ernst Ludwig to a professorship in Darmstadt the Viennese style was represented mainly by Josef Hoffmann and Koloman Moser who was a brilliant colorist and craftsman. Together with Otto Wagner, Gustav Klimt, Emil Orlik, Alfred Roller and Karl Moll, all of whom were members of the Wiener Werkstätte (founded 1905), they worked during the period 1905–1911 on the design of the epoch's foremost architectural achievement, the Palais Stoclet which had been commissioned by the Belgian industrialist. Josef Hoffmann was probably the first to have the audacity to completely dispense with the mirror frame. He designed a freestanding plate glass mirror with bevelled edges and black ebony base. The sole ornamentation consists of interlacing ellipses on the base (Ill. 289).

The main figures within the Sezession group (which was founded in Munich in 1892) specializing in interior decoration and furniture design were Hermann Obrist, who also attracted considerable attention at the Paris World Exhibition, Bruno Paul and Bernhard Pankok. Pankok designed a plain wall mirror in cherrywood with varying sections of marquetry as part of a bedroom suite for Dr. Krug (Ill. 284). One of the members of the Darmstadt artists' community, Mathildenhöhe, created a mirror in tin alloy with a highly original form reminiscent of jewelry design (Ill. 283).

The Belgian, Henry van de Velde (1865–1957), was very influential in the field of interior decoration. In 1901 he wrote in 'What I Desire': 'I strive to eradicate everything which debases decorative art by making it absurd, and I wish to replace outdated symbolical elements which we can no longer consider effective nowadays with a new and equally deathless beauty.' The furniture which he designed for Count Kessler and Julius Meier-Graefe demonstrate that ornamentation was no arbitrary matter to him, but instead was employed to emphasize the artistic aspect of furniture in accordance with the basic principle that all ornamental detail was to be derived from the work as a whole. Thus, although he continued to accept the cheval-glass as a valid form, he transformed it into a rectangular swivel dress mirror which was both very simple in form and highly practical (guest bedroom in the Kessler appartment in Weimar).

On the whole French Art Nouveau lacked a functionalist or reformist dimension. It was also prone to succumb to the demands of the world of luxury and representation. The movement of growing vegetation was employed to liberate architecture and handicrafts from the immobile solidity of static materials. This movement was itself designed to fulfil the function of ornamentation and even sculpture. Hector Guimard, who became famous for his Métro entrances in Paris, called himself an 'art architect'. A glass cabinet which Guimard designed in 1900 could be considered more a sculpture than an actual piece of furniture even though its function is still evident. Plant motifs were often presented in the form of flowing ornamental arcs. In Lille there is an overmantel mirror by Hector Guimard with the frame in the form of stems of plants which give the mirror an almost convex appearance while ornamental sections fill the spaces between the wooden spars. A synthesis of various art forms is thus reflected within this one piece of interior decoration (Colour Plate XIV). In his main work, the Castel Béranger appartment building in Paris, Guimard's most important quality, namely his dynamic feeling for form which creates his own special brand of flexible tension, finds its full expression.

The Nancy group consciously maintained the local rococo tradition of Jean Lamour and advocated a style based on a largely naturalistic use of plant motifs. The main figures in this group were Victor Prouvé, Louis Majorelle, Eugène Vallé and the glassmaker Emile Gallé, who all devoted a lot of attention to furniture design in accordance with their philosophy that all man-made objects ought to be designed to the last detail. Flowing, bountiful Nature was the great model and such motifs as grass stalks, tree roots, orchids, carnations, irises, callas, water lilies, marine life, dragon-flies, mermaids with flowing hair, weeping willows, waves, clouds, and indeed everything which could be subjected to the principle of dynamic form, were seized upon with enthusiasm and employed as symbolical vehicles for conveying mood in the style of Verlaine's poetic technique.

Despite the social and industrial principles which Art Nouveau claimed to embody artists like Guimard and Gallé were basically committed to an elitist concept of art. Proof of this can be seen in a wardrobe with mirror doors by Eugène Grasset (Ill. 277). The mass production of such Art Nouveau creations inevitably led to an intolerable lack of taste which the whole epoch indulged in for a long time. The Spaniard, Antonio Gaudi, occupies a special position within the movement in that he is regarded by many as a precursor of Expressionism. Relying on his own dynamic and eccentric individualism, he employed unusual materials and forms in his designs. As early as 1890 he designed a dressing table for the Güell Palace in Barcelona whose fluid lines are coupled with almost Surrealist alienation effects. The rectangular mirror is mounted at a slant with one edge sagging while the table legs suggest an upward spiralling movement (Ill. 286).

ART DECO

After the 1925 Paris World Exhibition, the 'Exposition Internationale des Arts Décoratifs et Industriels Modernes', Art Deco, as it was termed, emerged as a movement which, in contrast to Art Nouveau, argued that form and ornamentation should be subordinated to the question of function. This idea had already been advocated in 1900 by Adolf Loos and Francis Jourdain and put into practice by Hoffmann, the Wiener Werkstätte, Deutscher Werkbund (founded in 1907 by Hermann Muthesius), and the Bauhaus. But while an active quest for new principles of design developed in Germany after the First World War, the group of traditionalist Art Deco artists in France centred around Jacques Ruhlmann, Paul Follot, André Groult, Jules Leleu, Süe & Mare, Pierre Chareau, and Jean Dunand derived their inspiration from the ébénistes, the French cabinetmakers of the Ancien Régime in the late 18th century. Ruhlmann for example specifically mentioned Riesener and Weisweiler as being his models.

It can thus be argued that a last attempt was made in France to maintain traditional values in the field of design. Paul Follot rejected every form of mass production and insisted on the use of choice materials, richly carved ornamentation and sophisticated techniques. In Illustration 299 there is an exquisite dresser in blue lacquer with gold-leaf ornamentation, crowned by an oval mirror with carved garlands hanging on both sides. Ruhlmann himself designed a strikingly elegant dressing table. The circular swivel mirror is mounted on a fixture which like the table is made of Macassar ebony. One can also recognize the graceful decorative design on the table top in Ruhlmann's drawing (Ills. 307, 308). On the whole ebony played an important role in furniture design of the period together with Macassar ebony, palisander, palmwood, amaranth, maple wood and other rare kinds of wood. In addition the Oriental technique of lacquering became an integral part once more of the cabinetworker's repertoire. Exquisite marquetry was as popular a form of decoration as straw marquetry, and bas-reliefs in cast metal just as fashionable as costly ivory. In addition to exotic veneer woods, natural materials like shagreen and parchmentlike vellum paper also played a certain role. Snakeskin and pony skin also corresponded in texture to the taste of the period.

The Art Deco period attached great importance to the role of metal within the field of interior decoration and furniture design. Armand Albert Rateau preoccupied himself mainly with antique patinated bronze while Edgar Brandt from Alsace became the leading representative of contemporary wrought iron-work. A dressing table which mas made for Jeanne Lanvon in the period 1920–1922 is comparable in its structure to the one by Ruhlmann mentioned above, although it is much more richly decorated. It is lit by light bulbs set in daisy forms in the bronze mirror frame (Ill. 304). A wrought-iron mirror entitled 'Les Jets d'Eau' by Edgar Brandt (Ill. 301) was exhibited at the 1925 World Exhibition in the pavilion which had been designed by Ruhlmann under the title 'L'Hôtel du Collectioneur', and aroused great admiration at the time. Many exhibits were purchased directly by the Musée des Arts Décoratifs in Paris or the Metropolitan Museum of Art. It ought to be mentioned that rich clients played an important role as art patrons.

At Mrs Fellowes' suggestion the architect Louis Süe set about designing a room which was to create the impression of having no walls at all. As a result the room was completely panelled with mirrors which were accentuated by large surrounds of blue glass. The mercury silvering creates a very blurred artistic effect. Lady Mendl's bathroom with mirror panelling was designed in 1930 by Siclis the interior decorator. Mme. Jacques Lebel's bathroom in Folie St. James, which was also lined with mirrors, was decorated with parrots and monkeys by Dorian. Among other things Jansen designed a bathroom with mirror panelling for Mrs Biddle in Fontainebleau in which the tulip pattern decor by Charlemagne was intended to give the illusion of a blooming garden, Mme Henri de Jouvenel's bathroom, and Lady Castelrosse's dining room in mirror glass and stucco in Venice.

Max Ingrand and Lardin revived the technique of mirror engraving. Bolette Natanson used unusual combinations of different materials for his mirror frames: chromium-plated metal, perforated sheet-metal, lacquered wood, cork and parchment. Gilbert Poillcrat produced very artistic mirror frames in wrought iron. J. Hanau created costly fixé paintings. Mariano Andreü used coloured paper cut-outs and rolled cellophane to shape mirror frames which he then covered with parchment (Ill. 316). Tita Terrisse decorated mirrors with small irisdescent marbles and plaster ornaments in the shape of gloves and pipes.

For fifteen years Serge Roche also played an important role as artist and designer. At his exhibition in 1934 he presented obelisks, vases, dinner services, consoles, tables, dressers, fireplaces, chairs, and mirrors, and most of these were overlaid with faceted mirror glass. Among the most important exhibits were a fireplace in mirror glass with lead, crystal and seashell designs belonging to Mrs Fellowes, an enormous fireplace belonging to Countness Pastré, a baroque hallway obelisk by Salacron after a design by André Barsacq, large-size consoles from Mme Alfred Fabre-Luce's dining room, a wall clock with base for the Duke of Windsor and, last but not least, a large baroque obelisk with cut glass lamellas which was especially designed for a niche in the artist's own home and which Henri de Regnier termed the 'bell tower of Our Lady of the Mirrors'.

The conservative nature of the French society in the inter-war years ensured that high-quality handcrafted furniture, including mirrors, was granted a certain degree of continuity beyond the actual Art Deco period, a period which ought at any rate to be regarded as an integral part of the history of French interior decorating, despite the fact that this style was often imitated abroad and at times even copied cheaply as was the case in London. Cubist painting and sculpture had an obvious influence on Art Deco and often amalgamated with it in the sphere of interior decoration. Mirrors had an important function in those circles which cultivated refined and often exotic tastes. One of the favourite forms for wall mirrors was the oval shape with almost over-elongated dimensions, whilst numerous types of dressing tables in this period were mounted with a circular swivel mirror. The cheval-glass was once more able to gain a position of eminence within the fashion of the times (Ill. 306). The most significant commissions for artist craftsmen during this period were for the interior décor of the great luxury liners, the Ile de France, Lafayette, Atlantique, Normandie etc., which also served as floating exhibition pavilions for French arts and crafts.

As had already been the case in 1900, the 1925 World Exhibition not only gave Art Deco its name but also documented a style which was already past its peak. Apart from the initially limited success of the 'L'Esprit Nouveau' group around Le Corbusier, and of others like Robert Mallet-Stevens seeking to revive furniture design, the Bauhaus had scarcely any impact in France. Stylistic innovations only gained ground after René Herbst founded the Union des Artistes Modernes. A dressing table by René Herbst in chrome steel and glass (Ill. 310) reflects what was at issue in the controversy between the modernists and the so-called traditionalists, i.e. the use of metal in combination with glass in furniture design and a complete ban on ornamentation in so far as it was not a direct result of basic geometric forms. Only by means of such simplification and functionalism was it possible to establish mass production in furniture to satisfy the needs of modern industrial society and to resolve the contradiction between form and function.

Notes on the Illustrations

XIII. Psyche of Empress Eugénie. By Henri Fourdinois. France. 2nd half of 19th c.

XIV.   Overmantel mirror. By Hector Guimard. Lille, France. 1898–1900.

XV.   Dressing table mirror in silver. West Germany. About 1900.

XVI.   Dressing table. By Jacques Ruhlmann. France. 1925–1930.

and ears of corn. The frame is in carved wood. *Musée de Cluny.*

50, 51   Pocket-mirrors. 16th c.

50   Oval mirror in silvered glass, which Limoges enamel-work opposite. Case covered with leather. 0.14 × 0.11 m. Mirror in engraved copper gilt. On reverse, a cupid chases a peacock ('Love hates Pride'). Case, wood bordered with metal. 0.08 × 0.07 m. *Pierre Bernard.*

51   Mirrors encased in black leather. 0.10 × 0.08 m and 0.07 × 0.05 m. *Pierre Bernard.* Mirror with reverse in Limoges enamel. 0.10 × 0.06 m. *Brimo de la Roussilhe.*

52   Oval mirror in carved walnut. Louis XIII period. 2.20 × 1.40 m. The border illustrates the litanies of the Virgin. *J. Lebel.*

53, 54   Convex mirrors. Louis XIII period. Diam.: 0.16 m. Curved distorting mirrors. Borders of ebonized pearwood. Often used in physical laboratories. *S. Roche.*

55, 56   Mirror in carved gilt oak: 'Apollo and the Muses'. 17th c. (Louis XIII). 2 × 1.60 m. The Muses are shown singing, playing trumpet, oboe, lute, and tambourine. *Gruel.*

57, 58   Louis XIV mirror. Carved gilt wood, with pediment and mirror panels. Second half of 17th c. 1.65 × 0.85 m. Mouldings in the style of Bérain. *S. Roche and J. Rotil.*

59, 60   Louis XIV mirror. Carved gilt wood, with pediment and mirror panels. *c.* 1700. 2 × 1.04 m. Mouldings in Bérain style. *S. Roche and J. Rotil.*

61   Régence mirror of carved gilt wood, with panels of mirror. Early 18th c. 1.76 × 0.96 m. Decorated with reeds, rocks, flowers, shells and wings on pediment. *S. Roche and J. Rotil.*

62   Louis XIV mirror. *c.* 1700. 1.07 × 0.63 m. Border of carved gilt wood in Bérain style: stap-work, flowers, scrolls, palmettes. Triple candle brackets in gilt wrought iron. *S. Roche and J. Rotil.*

63   Louis XIV mirror with pediment in carved gilt wood and red lacquer decorated with gilt chinoiseries. Early 18th c. 1.75 × 1.05 m. *Javal.*

64   Louis XIV mirror with pediment in carved gilt wood and glass '*églomisé*' red. *c.* 1700. 2.76 × 1.47 m. Bérain style. *Musée des Arts Décoratifs.*

65   Régence mirror in carved gilt wood. 1.05 × 0.35 m. *J. Rotil.*

66   Louis XV mirror in carved gilt wood. 1 × 0.7 m. *S. Roche and J. Rotil.*

67, 68   Régence hand-mirror in bronze gilt. H.: 0.19 m. The disc is surmounted by a watch. On reverse, decoration in style of J. A. Meissonnier (1695–1750). No. 43 in S. R. Exhibition, 1934. *Mme Jules Strauss.*

69, 70   Louis XIV toilet-mirror with support. Early 18th c. 0,62 × 0,51 m. Border and support in bronze and tortoise. Boulle style. *N. Landau.*

71   Overmantel-mirror, Louis XV. 2.20 × 1.20 m. Carved gilt wood decorated with swags of leaves and flowers round moulding with wave decorations. *Bensimon.*

72   Toilet-mirror in silver. 18th c. 0.60 × 0.40 m. Part of toilet-case bearing arms of Duke of Cadoval. Made in 1739 by silversmiths Igonnet, Lebou and Faucher. Background of gaddrooning bordered with fine mouldings. Five rococo clasps. Arms on pediment. Appeared in 'French Art in the Eighteenth Century' Exhibition, Copenhagen, 1935. *Detroit Museum, U.S.A.* Formerly *J. Helft.*

73   Mirror from the Countess of Nord's dressing-table. Louis XVI period. 0.97 × 0.75 m. Replica of the 'Toilette de Vénus', presented by Marie-Antoinette to Grand-Duchess Feodorovna. Border in bisque (Sèvres) carved by Blaizot in 1782. Original in Palace of Pavlovsk. Replica here reproduced is in *Sèvres Factory.*

74   Louis XV pier-glass and console table. 1.45 × 0.65 m. Carved gilt wood, decorated with waves, reeds and palmettes. *Mme Tréfusis.*

75   Louis XV mirror framed in Strasbourg China. 0.85 × 0.50 m. Disorderly rococo style. Polychrome porcelain. *Musée de Strasbourg.* Formerly *Adolphe Lion.*

76   Pier-glass in carved wood. Painted gold and grey. Early 18th c. 2.08 m × 1.59 m. One can also recognize in the room an overmantel mirror from the same period. *Musée du Louvre, Paris.*

77   Louis XVI mirror with pediment, in carved and painted wood. 0.96 × 0.73 m. Border in two shades of gold on cream base, decorated with flowers, ribbons, and tassels. On pediment, dolphins and shells; on base, quivers and arrows; fleurs de lys in corners. *Private collection.*

78   Louis XVI mirror with pediment in carved wood. 0.80 × 0.40 m. Frame has Greek corners. Interlaced initials on base (A.M.). Contained in Louis XVI rosewood glass case. *Arturo Lopez-Willshaw.*

79   Patch-box of the Marchioness of Pompadour. 18th c. Bought by Lazare Duvaux at the Countess of Lauragais' sale for the Marchioness of Pompadour. Made in 1759, under the super-

vision of Richard, in gold and orange lacquer inlaid with small panels of black and gold lacquer. *Private collection.*

80, 81   Madame de Balbi's small leather case. Late 18th c. Gift of the Count of Provence. *Private collection.*

82, 84   Travelling cutlery-case. 18th c. Embossed leather case. *N. Landau.*

83   Small leather dressing-case in form of book. 18th c. Mirror and bottles. *N. Landau.*

85   Dressing-table of Marie-Antoinette whilst imprisoned in the *Temple. Musée Carnavalet.*

86   Mirrors from Marie-Antoinette's dressing-case. 1788–89. Silver. The rectangular mirror has a support. Round concave mirror, and ivory handle. The various pieces are enclosed in a chest of mahogany and copper by the cabinet marker, Palma. *Louvre.*

87   Silver travelling-case. Late 18th c. 0.56 × 0.39 m. Comprising 18 pieces in chest of mahogany and copper with 2 drawers holding 4 removable feet which can be screwed on to make a piece of furniture. *Hermès.*

88   Oval mirror in iron frame. Late 18th c. 0.35 × 0.28 m. Arms crested by count's crown, held by winged figures; frame decorated with oak-leaves. The mirror swings on a horizontal axis, and was probably intended to be fixed on a *barbière. Hermès.*

89   Sketch for Louis XVI dressing-table mirror sil silver plate. On surround, amorini, draperies, quivers. Anonymous sketch. *Musée des Arts Décoratifs.*

90   Trophy-shaped mirror. Late 18th c. 1.22 × 0.71 m. Carved gilt wood. Shield with eagles' heads forms mirror. *Duchesse de Talleyrand.*

91   Microscope (with mirror) in bronze gilt. About 1750. H.: 0.45 m. By Magny (who worked for the Duke of Chaulnes). Shagreen cover. *Pierre Bernard.*

92   Centre-piece in carved gilt wood and glass. Louis XV period. 0.44 × 0.34 m. Rococo style. Baroque obelisk form (French glass of early 17th c.). *S. Roche and J. Rotil.*

93   King Jérôme's toilet-case. Empire style. Mirror: 0.54 × 0.45 m. Ebony and plates of *verre églomisé.* Gilded bronze. On reverse, cypher of J. M. crowned. Made by Biennais. *M. Goffroy.*

94   Dressing-table in bird's-eye mahogany and bronze gilt. Empire. Mirror: 0.34 × 0.27 m. Marked G. Biennais. *Musée de Malmaison.*

95 Mirror 'à la Montgolfière', in carved gilt wood. Late 18th c. 1.59 × 0.92 m. *Paul de Montgolfier.*

96 Empress Marie-Louise's dressing-table in Vonèche crystal and bronze gilt. Early 19th c. 1.70 × 1.23 × 0.65 m. After a sketch by N. H. Jacob. Cut crystal mounted by Mme Désarnaud. It contains a small mechanical organ which plays a selection of 13 tunes. *Grognot and Joinel.*

97 Cheval-glass in mahogany and bronze. Empire. H.: 1.70 m. Standing on four lion's claws. Colonnettes supporting candlesticks and surmounted by vases. *Musée des Arts Décoratifs.*

98 Work-box in mother of pearl and bronze gilt. *c.* 1820. Artificial flowers on lid. Sewing accessoires in carved mother of pearl. *A la Vieille Russie.*

99 Queen Maria-Amelia's toilet-case. Early 19th c. 0.51 × 0.32 × 0.18 m. Made in silver-gilt by Aucoc the elder, comprising mirror and 19 pieces. *Hermès.*

100 Silver toilet-case. Early 19th c. 0.47 × 0.30 × 0.15 m. Chest in mahogany and copper. Made by Biennais. *Hermès.*

101 Toilet-case belonging to the Emperor of Brazil. 1827. 0.83 × 0.50 × 0.30 m. Made by Odiot. A mirror and 11 pieces in silver-gilt. Chest in Brazilian rose-wood and copper. Arms of don Pedro IV, King of Portugal, 1st Emperor of Brazil, appear on the lid. *Hermès.*

102 Mirror in gilt bronze. 'Troubadour' style. 1830–40. *Musée des Arts Décoratifs, Paris. Acc. No. 17673.*

103 Baccarat mirror. Late 19th. c. 1.17 × 0.70 m. Border of white bevelled glass. Corner-pieces and pediment in polychrome enamel on blue ground. Imitation of late 17th c. Venetian style. *S. Roche and J. Rotil.*

104 Palace of Maisons (Seine-et-Oise). Mirror room. Palace built by Mansart, *c.* 1650. Room listed in inventory of 1667. Round room with alternating pillars and mirror panels. Above, cupola with rich ornamentation. On stylobate, initials of owners, René de Longueil and Madeleine de Boulenc. Floor in wood and pewter. Restored in 1956 by J. Ch. Moreux, chief architect of the Palais Nationaux.

105 Versailles. War Drawing-Room. 10 × 10 m. Last work of Le Brun (1686). Two of the three false doors are of mirror.

106, 107 Hall of mirrors at Versailles. Built by Mansart, completed in 1684. Illuminated by 17 arched windows to which correspond seventeen archways, each containing 18 mirrors —

a total of 306 mirrors. The mirrors are bevelled, and set in bronze gilt moulding.

108 Bathroom of Hôtel de Beauharnais, Paris. Empire. Pompeian style. Walls of mirror plate, colonnettes painted imitation marble and surmounted by capitals decorated with dolphins. Bath in marble and bronze. The mansion was built in 1714 by G. Boffrand for the Marquis de Torcy.

Holland: 109–114

109 Overmantel-mirror in carved gilt wood. 17th c. 1 × 1.15 m. The carving stands out from the red-painted ground. Interlaced letters W and O on pediment. *S. Roche and J. Rotil.*

110 Toilet-mirror. Lutma style. 17th c. 0.70 × 0.45 m. Carved gilt wood. Toilet articles (brush, scissors, jewel-box, pin-tray, small mirror, etc.) form auricular decoration, on flat ground of frame. *Rijksmuseum, Amsterdam.*

111 Toilet-mirror. Lutma style. 17th c. 0.65 × 0.44 m. Carved gilt wood. Flat ground of frame has auricular ornamentation and garlands. On pediment, arms borne by two lions. *Rijksmuseum, Amsterdam.*

112 Mirror in bronze gilt and steel. Early 18th c. 0.70 × 0.47 m. Cartouches at corners and mid-points of frame coupled by garlands. On pediment, two lions and two amorini bear arms. *A. Hamelle.*

113 Mirror in carved gilt wood. 17th c. 0.75 × 0.54 m. Signs of Zodiac. Traces of polychrome. Inner moulding is guilloched. *Gruel.*

114 Mirror with frame of blue and white Delft-ware. 17th c. 0.75 × 0.48 m. Medley of scrolls, Virtues, amorini, and monsters. Large leaves at corners. *Rijksmuseum, Amsterdam.*

Germany and Central Europe: 115–166

115, 116 Wall-mirror in carved wood. Germany? 16th c. 1.50 × 0.90 m. Symbolic statuettes, death's-heads, amorini, in a complicated construction of scroll-work. Inscriptions in Dutch. *National Bavarian Museum, Munich.*

117, 118 Standing mirror in carved ivory and silver-gilt. 0.30 × 0.10 m. Made in Munich during last years of 16th c. by Christoph Angermeier. It is double-faced. On obverse of pedestal, enamelled arms; on back of mirror, small curved mirrors. *Arturo Lopez-Willshaw. Formerly Olsen.*

119, 120 Mirror in carved gilt wood. Late 18th c. 0.45 × 0.50 m. Large shells decorate crest and base; on each side, figures and horses emerge from the moulding. *Mme Tréfusis.*

121 Mirror in iron frame. 16th c. 0.60 × 0.50 m. *Private collection.*

122 Mirror in Dresden china frame. 18th c. 0.58 × 0.40 m. Curved border of porcelain with polychrome rococo decoration. No. 63 at S.R. Exhibition, 1934. *Formerly Ladislas collection.*

123 Mirror in cut glass and gilt wood. Germany. Early 17th c. The "precious stones" are offset from one another by silver crosspieces. Probably made in Halle. 1.05 × 0.85 m. *S. Roche.* See also Colour Plate X.

124 Detail of mirror in cut glass and gilt wood shown in ill. 123 and Colour Plate X.

125 Mirror in carved gilt wood and engraved glass. Austria, 18th c. 1.65 × 0.90 m. Pediment richly ornamented with heads, vases, trellis, and volutes. *S. Ex. M. Aguire, Madrid.*

126 Mirror in carved gilt wood and engraved glass. Hungary, 18th c. 1.70 × 0.85 m. *S. Ex. M. Aguire, Madrid.*

127 Mirror in polychrome faience frame. Rococo style. 18th c. 0.75 × 0.57 m. Arms on pediment. *Musée Carnavalet.*

128 Hand-mirror with singing bird. Made by Rochat brothers. Switzerland, *c.* 1818. 0.29 × 0.16 m. Weight 1 kg. Gold and enamel. On reverse, medaillion bordered with scrolls and decorated with landscape painting (Constantinople?). The mirror is surrounded by a garland of chased gold surmounted by a flower of gold with six petals which, when they open, reveal the bird. The mechanism is in the thickness of the mirror. The trigger is the small hook above the handle. The knob on the end of the handle is the winder. Made for Turkey. Appeared in 'Horloges et Automates' Exhibition at the Conservatoire des Arts et Métiers, 1954. *Sandoz, Switzerland.*

129 Engraved mirror pediment. Rococo style. Austria, 18th c. 1.60 × 0.74 m. The small mirrors are held by a narrow lead border. *Private collection, U.S.A.*

130 Mirror with pediment. The frame is in engraved glass in Rocaille style and in the Venetian tradition. Austria. 19th c. *Private collection, Vienna.*

131 Mirror in silver, silver-gilt, tortoise-shell and engraved glass. Marked Augsburg, 1699. Silver medallions represent amorous subjects (lady with fontange head-dress, man on his knees, couple in park) or mythological ones (Diane, Amphitrite). 2 × 1.12 m. Was seen as item No. 306 in 'Chefs-d'œuvre de la curiosité du monde' Exhibition, 1954 (Pavillon de Marsan). *Seligmann.*

132 Design for mirror room. By architect Paulus Decker. Etching by Johann Jacob Kleinschmid in 1711 for a King of Bavaria. 'This room may be decorated with a multitude of mirrors all round the walls, and with gilt mouldings, or porcelain, or all sorts of coloured glass. The ornamentation of the grottos may be gilded, and all kinds of tea-services or other vessels may be placed there. The grottos must be similarly covered with mirrors, and in hidden places, in hollows, lights may be placed where they cannot be seen, only reflected in the mirrors so as to create marvellous images. The cascades and water-falls are to be composed of water containing various perfumes. The grotesque heads may be so contrived that they give out through eyes and mouth beams of light which illuminate amusing texts, whenever a hidden mechanism is touched with the foot. Further, it should be noted that the oval mirrors will be made in such a way that faces become distorted, lengthways or sideways.' *S. Roche.*

133 Royal Palace of Charlottenburg (West-Berlin). China room. After a design by Eosander von Göthe. 1706. Several piedouches in gilded wood hold vases and plates of Chinese porcelain.

134–138 Palace of Pommersfelden (Bavaria). Mirror room. About 4 × 7 m. After a design by Ferdinand Plitzner. 1714–1719. Rich decoration of carved gilt wood in Louis XIV style on background of walnut and mirror plate. Several piedouches in gilded wood, some with candle branches, hold Chinese porcelain. Cornice with lambrequins, ceiling in stucco and mirror glass on blue ground. Floor walnut inlaid with ebony, copper and pewter.

139–147, 150 Residence of 'La Favorite' near Rastatt (Baden-Wurttemberg).

139–142, 144, 150 The mirror room. After a design by decorators Franz Pfleger and Hans Georg Stöhr in 1715. About 5 × 5 m. See description on page 36.

143, 145 Drawing-room or small dining-room. Mirrors with corners cut off surmounted by baroque ceiling in carved gilt wood. Curved mirrors in ceiling increase light from chandeliers.

146, 147 Florentine room. About 5 × 5 m. See description on page 37.

148, 149 Amalienburg Residence in park of Nymphenburg Palace (Bavaria). Large mirror room, after a design by architect François Cuvilliés, 1739. Stucco-work by J. B. Zimmermann. See description on page 37.

150, 151 Mirror drawing-room of Amalienburg Residence, near Munich. Designed by François Cuvilliés. Large mirrors in rococo style, carved silvered wood borders on blue ground. Ceiling decorated with silvered stucco, by Zimmermann, 1739.

152 Munich Residence (Bavaria). Royal room. After a design by F. Cuvilliés. 1731–33. Trumeau of mirror and carved gilt wood.

153 Munich Residence. Mirror room after a design by the architect François Cuvilliés. 1731–33.

·154 Würzburg Residence (Bavaria). Mirror room. After a design by J. W. von der Auvera. 1742–45. Rich decoration of carved gilt wood and painted mirror glass in Chinese style, and in European style on walls, wainscot and doors. Ceiling of mirrors and gilded stucco in Chinese style. Stucco by Antonio Bossi. This palace was partially destroyed during the last war.

155–158 Royal Palace of Ludwigsburg (Wurttemberg). Mirror room. After a design by architect Friedrich Nette. 1716. Room composed of bedroom and antichamber, both square (about 4 × 4m.) joinded by large bay. Rich decoration in wood and gilt stucco, framing mirrors on light green ground.

155, 156 Bedroom ceiling of stucco and mirrors, supported by high richly decorated cornice.

157, 158 Antichamber. Ill. 157 shows springing of soffit on dividing pilaster. Ill. 158 shows ceiling, with stucco by Donato Frisoni.

159, 160 Ansbach Residence. Mirror room. After a design by P. A. Biarelle, 1739. The original arrangement in French style (mirror panels in white and gold frames) has almost disappeared. The decoration was considerably overcrowded when the number of pier-tables was almost doubled so as to exhibit a greater number of porcelain pieces. Panelling carved by J. K. Wezler.

161, 162 Hermitage Palace near Bayreuth (Bavaria). Residence built for the Margrave Wilhelmina, sister of Frederick the Great. 1715–1718. Enlarged 1735. Decoration of mirrors and panels lacquered in shades of beige.

163, 164 New Palace of Bayreuth. Mirror room. Stucco by J. B. Pedrozzi. 1755. Rococo style. In the midst of clouds and dragons of gilt stucco strewn with variously shaped mirrors, Chinese figures with long tresses pay homage to the Goddess Kuan Yin.

165 Cupola of Zwiefalten church. Mid-18th c. Small fragments of mirror are inlaid in the rococo stucco adorning the pendentives of the cupola.

166 Round chapel, Andechs (Bavaria). Mid-18th c. Small fragments of mirror inlaid in stucco.

Great Britain, United States: 167–203

167, 168 Mirror with pediment. Late 17th c. 1.75 × 0.90 m. Blue and white glass border with leaf decoration. *S. Roche.*

169 Mirror frame with marquetry. Late 17th c. *Victoria and Albert Museum, London.*

170 Three sconces and mirror. Late 17th and early 18th c. *Lieut.-Colonel L. Jenner.*

171 Gilt mirror frame. Queen Anne period. *Lieut.-Colonel L. Jenner.*

172, 173 Dressing-table mirror with Stumpwork decoration. Mid-17th c. 1.20 × 1.05 m. Embroidery in slight relief, bordered with galons. *Mme Tréfusis.*

174 Dressing-table mirror framed in silver-plated copper. 17th c. 0.60 × 0.45 m. On pediment a flaming heart surrounded by two amorini; two more amorini support the mirror. The whole amid scrolls, foliage and coquillage. *Mme Tréfusis.*

175 Mirror in carved gilt wood by Grinling Gibbons (1648–1721). 2.05 × 1.50 m. *Victoria and Albert Museum.*

176 Mirror frame in the style of Grinling Gibbons (1648–1721).

177 Rectangular mirror as fireside decor. Late 17th c. England. *Hampton Court Palace.*

178 Mirror with gilt frame in Chippendale style. Approx. 1755. *Worshipful Company of Carpenters.*

179 Mirror in red and gold lacquer. 18th c. 1.30 × 0.40 m. Frame decorated with chinoiseries. Star engraved on mirror. *N. Landau.*

180 Mirror framed in engraved glass and gilt wood. Early 18th c. 1.93 × 0.70 m. Fine engravings on join between mirror plates. *Duchesse de Talleyrand.*

181 Mirror in black and gold lacquer. Early 18th c. 1.80 × 0.60 m. Frame decorated with chinoiseries. Fine engravings on join between mirror plates. *Duchesse de Talleyrand.*

182 Mirror framed in gilt gesso. Early 18th c. 1.20 × 0.66 m. Broken pediment, palmettes and flames. Bronze sockets supporting candle brackets. *Duchesse de Talleyrand.*

183 Mirror in gilt wood. Early 18th c. 1.65 × 0.84 m. Palmettes and volutes on pediment; on the base, palmettes, scrolls and foliage. *Duchesse de Talleyrand.*

184 Mirror framed in gilt wood and walnut. Early 18th c. 1.22 × 0.66 m. Broken pediment, shells and foliage. Sockets of bronze gilt for candle brackets. *Duchesse de Talleyrand.*

185 Mirror framed in carved gilt wood and blue glass. Early 18th c. 1.72 × 0.86 m. On pediment, interlaced letters between volutes; shell on base. *Duchesse de Taleyrand.*

186 Small secretary with toilet-glass in lacquer. Early 18th c. 1.62 × 0.84 m. The swing-mirror rests on small writing-desk with four feet. Yellow and green lacquer. Decorated with flowers in Chinese style. *Musée des Arts Décoratifs.*

187 Toilet-table in satinwood. Late 18th c. *James Thursby-Pelham.*

188 Toilet-table. Late 18th c.

189, 191, 192 Mirror in gilt wood. Chinese manner. Chippendale style. Mid-18th c. 2 × 1.30 m. Amid the rococo openwork one can see flowers and birds. On the pediment, a Chinese woman combing her hair before a small dressing-table. Reproduced in Chippendale's etchings, *c* 1760. *H. R. H. Duke of Windsor.*

190 Overmantel-mirror in carved gilt wood. Chippendale style. 18th c. Above a pagoda, on either side small pagoda surmounted by bird. *Former collection Serge Roche and J. Rotil.*

193 Dressing-case in gold and engraved glass. Early 18th c. In the form of a miniature escritoire with watch in pediment. Dark green leather, rococo decoration in chased gold. Panels of engraved rock-crystal, lined with silver foil, representing Diana, Flora, Apollo in his chariot, and Amphitrite with two hippocampi. The case contains several toilet accessories, including a mirror. On the back of the watch, arms (in enamel) of the Margrave Ludwig-Wilhelm of Baden and the Duchess Augusta of Saxe Altenburg, who were married in 1690. '*A la Vieille Russie*'. Formerly *Baroness Mathilda von Rotschild (Frankfurt).*

194 Dance card in gold and agate. *c.* 1750. Rococo style. Appeared in Goldschmidt-Rotschild sale, Berlin, 1933. '*Au Vieux Paris*'.

195 Dressing-case in gold and red ribbon agate. H.: 0.23 m. On the lid, a small watch signed John Best, who worked in London about 1750. '*A la Vieille Russie*'.

196 Pocket-mirror in case. Gilt and silvered bronze. 18th c. 0.10 × 0.08 m. Filigree work. Arms in centre. *N. Landau.*

197 Painted mirror in bevelled glass frame. 18th c. 0.38 × 0.33 m. Appliqué iron ornaments at corners. *Mme H. Gonse.*

198 Mirror framed in cut glass. 18th c. 0.65 × 0.40 m. Dressing-table mirror with pediment. Engraved, bevelled glass. *Mme Tréfusis.*

199 Girandole mirror in carved gilt sprucewood. England. 1800. Height approx. 0.92 m. *Brooklyn Museum, New York. Acc. No. 60.136.1.*

200 Mirror with engraved glass pediment. 18th c. 0.75 × 0.35 m. Bevelled and engraved blue and white glass. *Mme Tréfusis.*

201 Mirror framed in painted wood and cut glass. Early 19th c. Ext. diam.: 1.50 m. Round mirror girdled with garter. Carved motto. Radiating beams of plated glass. *Mrs. Kemp.*

202 Convex mirror in gilt wood. Late 18th or early 19th c. 2.15 × 1.65 m. The curved mirror is framed in carved wood, gilded and painted in Adam style. Laterally, two serpents forming candle brackets. Originally in Brighton Pavilion. *Jansen.*

203 Toilet-mirror. Furniture, frame and pediment in solid walnut in the style of the American Renaissance of the 19th c. By Thomas Brooks & Company, Brooklyn. 1870–80. Height: approx. 2.70 m. *Brooklyn Museum, New York Acc. No. 45.25.2.*

Italy: 204–248

204, 206 Mirror in iron damascened with gold. 16th c. 0.38 × 0.24 m. Figures in architectural decoration. Spitzer sale, June 1893. *Coll. Dutuit. Musée du Petit Palais.*

205 Mirror with mermaids. 15th c. 1.20 × 1.80 m. Carved gilt wood. *Cà d'Oro, Venice.*

207 Octagonal mirror. Marble and bronze gilt. 16th. c. 0.90 × 0.52 m. *Musée de Cluny.*

208 Mirror in bronze gilt. 16th c. 0.25 × 0.15 m. Figures and heads in strapwork motif. *A. Lopez-Willshaw.*

209 'Mermaid with Mirror', attributed to Benvenuto Cellini (1555). Pearl, ruby, topaz. Height: 0.08 m. Presented to a Mogul Emperor of India by a Medici prince. It is shown in the portrait of a Medici princess (painter unknown). Discovered in the treasury of the King of Oudh at the capture of Delhi by the British. Exhibited at the South Kensington Museum in 1862, at the Fogg Art Museum in 1937, at the Cleveland Museum of Art in 1947, and the Portland Art Museum in 1952. *Arturo Lopez-Willshaw; formerly in following collections: Lord Canning, K.G., Viceroy of India; Julius Goldschmidt of Frankfurt; Baroness Mathilde von Rotschild (Frankfurt); Baron Max von Goldschmidt Rotschild.*

210 'Mermaid with Mirror'. See note to ill. 209.

211 Standing mirror. Bronze and '*verre églomisé*'. 16th c. H.: 0.34 m. Frame of chased and gilded bronze. Reverse in *verre églomisé*. Was item No. 286 in 'Cabinet de l'Amateur' Exhibition, 1956, at the Orangerie. *P. Delbée.*

212 Leonardo's pocket-mirror. Ivory and silver. 1500. The inscription (silver on ivory) may be translated, 'Complain not of me, O Woman, for I render to you only what you give me.' The anagram of this sentence gives in Latin: 'Et Leonardo da Vinci geminet Leonardo da Vinci habent q mihi.' M.D. ('Let Leonardo da Vinci duplicate Leonardo da Vinci, and both are dumfounded, 1500.') *Michel de Bry.* Formerly *Jubinal de Saint-Albin.*

213 Mirror in carved gilt wood. 18th c. 2.20 × 1.40 m. Several small mirrors bordered by rococo decoration, garlands, vases, figures and animals. Harvesting scenes. On pediment, bust of man. *Private collection.*

214 Mirror with pediment. Cut glass. Venice, late 17th c. 1.10 × 0.75 m. Blue and white cut glass screwed to wooden back. Cable-moulding of glass thread. *P. Devinoy.*

215 Mirror in carved gilt wood with engraved female figure. 18th c. *Private collection, France.*

216 Mirror with candle brackets. Turin, 18th c. 1.30 × 0.60 m. Baroque style. Carved gilt wood. Female sphinxes, and grotesque masks coupled by garlands. The six candle brackets are of carved gilt wood. *S. Roche.*

217, 218 Engraved glass mirrors in gilt wood frame. Genoa, late 17th or early 18th c. 2.30 × 1.48 m. Breast-plates, flags, coquillages, flowers and scrolls. Mirror glass engraved with foliage. *S. Roche and J. Rotil.*

219, 220 Mirror framed in gilt wood and engraved glass. Venice, early 18th c. 2.45 × 1.60 m. Border decorated with scrolls, foliage, garlands and mascarons, surrounding engraved glass representing women — one is looking in a hand-mirror — animals and trophies. *S. Roche and J. Rotil.*

221 Mirror framed in gilt wood decorated with engraved white and blue glass. Venice, 18th c. 1.60 × 1.30 m. The white glass is engraved with garlands, medallions, and ribbons. Cabochons of blue glass are screwed to the mouldings of gilt wood. *Formerly S. Roche.*

222 Overmantel mirror, gilt wood. Venice, 18th c. 0.95 × 1.30 m. The joins between the three mirrors are covered by moulding. *S. Roche and J. Rotil.*

223 Dressing-case in pale blue lacquer. Venice, 18th c. 0.55 × 0.40 × 0.22 m. Decoration of polychrome flowerets. The toilet articles date from 19th c. *S. Roche and J. Rotil.*

224 Mirror in carved gilt wood and green lacquer. Venice, 18th c. 2.60 × 1.50 m. *Palazzo Rezzonico.*

225, 226 Monumental mirror with gilt polychrome carved frame. 18th c. 2.35 × 1.50 m. N. Italy. Surrounded by paintings of landscapes; on the base, picture symbolizing the Arts and the Sciences. In pediment, round mirror surrounded by two statuettes and trophies of carved gilt wood which stand out from a rocky landscape of carved polychrome wood, in which is set a group of tents. An optical standing mirror can be seen in the lower picture. *Giorgini.*

227 Mirror in carved gilt wood and green lacquer. Venice, 18th c. 2.50 × 1.50 m, *Palazzo Rezzonico.*

228 Mirror in frame of '*églomisé*' glass. Venice, 18th c. 0.55 × 0.40 m. Decoration of bistre scrolls. Cable-moulding of glass thread round glass panels. *Private collection.*

229 Mirror framed in engraved glass with ornaments of blow glass. Venice, 18th c. 0.85 × 0.45 m. The glass candle brackets are missing. *Formerly S. Roche.*

230 Engraved mirror and gilt wood. Venice, 18th c. 0.60 × 0.40 m. The rococo ornamentation forms two 'ears' on each side. *Prince Aly Khan.*

231 Engraved mirror and Venetian glass. 18th c. 0.80 × 0.50 m. Engraving of masked woman and mirror. Polychrome ornaments of blown glass on frame and pediment. On base, three candle brackets of blown glass. *Mme Tréfusis.*

232 Mirror of gilt wood, blue glass and rock-crystal. Venice, 18th c. 0.95 × 0.65 m. Border of blue glass and gilt wood. On the mirror, a vase of flowers in rock-crystal is screwed. *Private collection.*

233 Mirror in yellow lacquer. Venice, 18th c. 1.80 × 1.10 m. Carved lacquered wood decorated with polychrome flowers. *Private collection.*

234 Dressing-table mirror in black and gold lacquer. Venice, 18th c. 0.71 × 0.45 m. Carved wood, gilt decoration in Chinese style. Support (*valet*) at back. *Mme H. Gonse.*

235, 236 Mirror with pediment. Venetian glass and engraving. Late 18th c. 2.20 × 1.80 m. Twisted mouldings of drawn glass. On pediment, Justice. *Formerly Lady Mendl.*

237 Mirror framed in Venetian glass and engraved glass. 19th c. 2.25 × 1.15 m. Oval mirror of engraved glass, bordered with twisted moulding of glass thread, decorated with flowers and knots. Asymmetrical pediment. *Hall of Hotel Plaza, Paris.*

238–240 Chapel of former St. Philip's Monastery, Palermo. Early 18th c. Above the panelling, decoration of mirror panels topped by lambrequin of gilt wood, in which are set oval or curved niches of tortoise-shell with gilt pediments. Altar of gilded wood on ground of mirror glass. Five small reliquary-cases framed with tortoise-shell. *Now in the National Museum, Paris.*

241–244 Palazzo Terzi, Bergamo. 18th c. Room of mirrors and gilt wood. Above the panelled wainscot, everything is composed of mirror glass. On the glass walls are large mirror-frames, candle brackets with plaques, entablature of mirror plate; on the ceiling the paintings are framed with glass and gilt wood.

245 Borromeo Palace. Chapel. Isola bella. Lake maggiore. Mirror and gilt wood. Engraved mirrors on ceiling. 18th c.

246 Royal Palace of Stupinigi. 18th c. Hunting residence of the Dukes of Savoy. Work of Juvara. Drawing-room (about 5 × 5 m.) decorated with large mirrors framed with gilt wood alternating with panels of silk, in frames of pierced gilt wood, inlaid with small fragments of glass which also decorated the door-casings. On the ceiling, rococo stucco framing small pieces of glass.

247, 248 Palazzo Litta, Milan. 18th c. In the state drawing-room (10 × 15 m.) of this fine rococo palace, *trompe-l'oeil* painting has been introduced. Upper walls, ceiling, and lower panelling, doors, windows, paintings, and large mirrors in gilt wood with fretted pediments, all form a single composition. In the small octagonal drawing-room, large mirrors in carved gilt wood. Ceiling, stucco.

Spain: 249–258

249–253 Guadalupe Convent (New Castile).

251, 252 Octagonal mirror with pediment. Bronze gilt and rock-crystal. Early 18th c. 1.30 × 1.55 m. Recessed, receding section. Very ornate mouldings of bronze gilt (grotesque heads at corners) in which are set mirrors partly covered by the network of rock-crystal, in the form of flowers, rosettes, and water-droplets.

249, 250 Similar mirrors to preceding. 1.20 × 1.40 m.

253 El Camarin. 18th c. room, divided into four hemicycles. Round the pictures by Luca Giordano, the walls are entirely covered with gilt wood and mirrors painted with tulips, roses, birds, and angels' heads in the scrolls.

254 Octagonal mirror. Gilt wood and painted glass. Early 17th c. 0.88 × 0.80 m. Recessed mouldings of carved gilt wood adorned with fruit and foliage. Small panels of painted glass (roses, anemones, tulips) surrounded by guilloched moulding.

255 Mirror in carved gilt wood. Early 18th c. 1.20 × 0.80 m. Strongly marked carving. Gilding covered by rich polychrome. *Villanova.*

256 Gilt wood mirror. Early 18th c. 1.27 × 1.12 m. Frame decorated with small pieces of mirror surrounded with cemented hemp. Moorish influence. *Formerly S. Roche.*

257, 258 Cathedral altar, Salamanca. Carved gilt wood and mirror. 18th c. 'Christ scourged' by Carmona.

Portugal: 259–269

259 Triple mirror, carved mahogany inlaid with lemon-wood. Late 18th c. 1.27 × 1.40 m. On the pediment, baskets full of flowers, garlands and birds in carved mahogany. *Gruel.*

260 Dressing-case in tortoise-shell and silver. 18th c. H.: 0.24 m. Comprises mirror framed with tortoise-shell and silver, and a comb. *N. Landau.*

261–269 Royal Palace of Queluz (near Lisbon). 18th c. See description on page 39.

262 Detail of altar in carved gilt wood and mirror. 18th c. Now in Lisbon Museum.

ART NOUVEAU: 270–295

270 Small wall mirror in carved limewood with delicate hues. Art Nouveau. France. 1900. 0.39 × 0.27 m. *Kunstgewerbemuseum, West Berlin. Acc. No. 66.10.*

271 Hand mirror in the stylized form of a peacock. Form influenced by Tiffany. The bird's arched neck forms the handle while the feathers on the back of the mirror consist of coloured enamel and sapphires. *Museum of Modern Art, New York.*

272 Hand mirror for the dressing table by Webster, Picadilly. Cast in bronze. Patinated

and lacquered. Leaf-shaped base with female figure emerging. Height: 0.32 m. England. 1900. *Museum Bellerive, Zurich.*

273, 274 Hand mirror by Vever. 1889. An antique robed figure with wings forms the handle. On the back of the mirror (Ill. 274) Narcissus kneels at a pool regarding his reflection. Opposite to him the rock where Echo the water nymph sits. Above the scene is a stylized narcissus. Greek inscriptions complete the impression of antiquity. Height: 0.26 m; diameter: 0.13 m. *Musée des Arts Décoratifs, Paris. Acc. No. 24483.*

275 Handmirror. By Vever. 1889. A mermaid with plated tail ensconced in conch forms the handle while the frame is decorated with seaweed motif and snail. Height: 0.25 m; diameter: 0.12 m.

276 Hand mirror. By Ernst Moritz Geyger. 1897. The figure of the youth is modeled on Ancient Greek themes. The back of the mirror shows a naked female figure who has been wounded by Cupid's arrows. Height: 0.15 m; diameter: 0.09 m. *Museum für Kunst und Gewerbe, Hamburg. Acc. No. 1900.251.* (A further copy was made for Empress Auguste Victoria of Germany.)

277 Wardrobe with mirror doors by Eugène Grasset. France 1900. *Gal. Brockstedt, Hamburg.*

278 Mirror frame with consoles in leaf design. By Louis Majorelle. Nancy, France. 1898. Carved walnut with leaf decor and leaf-shaped consoles. This piece of work consciously identifies itself with the elegant rococo tradition of the late 18th c. 2.55 × 1.25 × 0.21 m. *Mittelrheinisches Landesmuseum Mainz. Acc. No. 75/182.*

279 Wall mirror. By Barend Jordens. Frame in carved untreated wood. Represents 'The Vale of Tears'. Rectangular frame inscribed within basic lozenge-shaped form. Transition period between Dutch Nouveau and Art Deco. 1918. Height 0.90 m.

280 Table mirror from the Tiffany Studios. Oval swivel mirror with bronze fixture. Stand is in the form of waterlilies. Signed 'Tiffany Studios New York 29238'. 1900. Height: 0.50 m. *Christie, Manson & Woods International Inc.*

281 Mirror with frame in enamelled silver. Made by Hutton & Sons Ltd., Birmingham, England. 1902–03. On the lower face side are the firm's stamp, an English lion and the year mark. Linear decor with bluish green enamel inlays at the corners. *Museum Bellerive, Zurich. Acc. No. 1971.8.*

282 Dressing table. By Richard Riemerschmid. 1898. Untreated walnut. 1.92 × 0.69 m. *Bayrisches Nationalmuseum, Munich Acc. No. SW 123.*

283 Mirror frame in tin alloy. Stamped AK & Cie. 1902. 0.52 × 0.27 m. *Private collection Ludwig Endner, Darmstadt.*

284 Wall mirror (crystal glass) in cherrywood with marquetry. By Bernhard Pankok. 1902. Part of the bedroom designed for Dr. Krug, 1900–02. Manufacturer: Vereinigte Werkstätten, Munich. The mirror is signed '1902 BP' on the inlay section. 0.84 × 0.54 m. *Galerie Kenneth Barlow, Munich.*

285 Wall mirror with console table. 1.72 × 0.56 m. In front is an Art Nouveau candle-stick. Nancy School. 1900. *Private collection, France.*

286 Dressing table. By Antonio Gaudi. 1890. Designed for the Güell Palace in Barcelona. This piece stands apart from Art Nouveau and demonstrates Gaudi's personal world of phantasy.

287 Dressing table. France. Manufacturer: Plumet & Selmersheim. The table legs form console-shaped shelves. The mirror is in three parts and adjustable. *Museum für Kunst und Gewerbe, Hamburg.*

288 Dressing table. By Franz Messner. Vienna. 1900. In stained, polished maple wood. Bevelled glass in brass frame with copper mountings. Manufacturer: Wenzel Hollmann. The table's design was influenced by the Glasgow School. 1.26 × 0.75 m. Depth: 0.56 m.

289 Full-length mirror. Vienna. 1908. Design by Josef Hoffmann. Bevelled glass mounted on wooden stand. Base in ebony veneer. The design is classical in its simplicity. 1.69 × 1.26 m. *Österreichisches Museum für Angewandte Kunst, Vienna. Acc. No. H 2075.*

290 Sideboard. By Fritz Zeymer. Vienna. 1908. Grained walnut veneer. Shelf and back are in white marble and the mirror is in a gilt frame with cloud decor. An unobtrusively elegant piece of furniture from the Wiener Werkstätte. 1.83 × 2.13 m. *Österreichisches Museum für Angewandte Kunst, Vienna. Acc. No. H 2057.*

291 Mirror frame. By Sigmund Jaray. Vienna. 1899. In untreated wood. Lower edge is curved. Decor consists of circles and vertical grooves. *Österreichisches Museum für Angewandte Kunst, Vienna. Acc. No. H 957.*

292 Mirror frame in pearwood. Winter-cherries carved in relief. The flowers have light hues and the background is embossed. An apprentice piece by the woodcarver Franz Viehweider for the technical college in Bozen. 1901. 0.30 ×

0.44 m. *Österreichisches Museum für Angewandte Kunst, Vienna. Acc. No. H 959.*

293 Mirror frame in carved mahogany. Design by Josef Hoffmann. Diameter: 0.44 m; glass: 0.35 m. Before 1928. *Auktion W. Hassfurther, Vienna (31.1.1984).*

294 Table mirror in carved mahogany with ivory flower decor. Design by Josef Hoffmann. Diameter: 0.29 m; glass: 0.23 m. Before 1928. *Auktion W. Hassfurther, Vienna (31.1.1984).*

295 Mirror frame in carved walnut. Design by Josef Hoffmann. Diameter: 0.36 m; glass: 0.35 m. Before 1928. *Auktion W. Hassfurther, Vienna (31.1.1984).*

ART DECO: 296–316

296 Dining room with ceiling-high mirror sunk in wall cavity. In front is large ebony sideboard. Design by Jules Leleu (1883–1961) for the 1925 Paris World Exhibition. A classical and even Antique idiom reasserts itself in this piece.

297 Living-room furniture by Dominique and Alfred Porteneuve. Armchairs, sofa and table are in exotic wood and the long oval mirror has a gilt frame. Approx. 1925–30. *Private collection, France.*

298 Wall console in wrought iron with marble top and puma figure. Design by Raymond Subes. Above it hangs an oval mirror between two frame sections reminiscent of cornucopias. Approx. 1925–1930. *France.*

299 Chest of drawers in ultramarine lacquer. Moulding and central ornamental motif in leaf-gilding. Above it hangs an oval mirror in gilt wood with flower garlands on both sides. Design by Paul Follot (1877–1941). In this piece Art Deco is obviously continuing the traditions of the French ébénistes. *Fondation Helen Follot Vendel.*

300 Chest of drawers in figwood with decorative moulding in ebony and ivory and handles in silver-plated bronze. Above it hangs a ceiling-high mirror with rectangular panelling which also covers the pediment surface. Design by Paul Follot (1877–1941). His emblem, the rose, also appears in the carpet design. Approx. 1925–30. *Foundation Helen Follot Vendel.*

301 'Les Jets d'Eau'. Wrought-iron mirror by Edgar Brandt. Exhibited in 1925 in the 'Hotel du Collectionneur', the pavilion designed and decorated by Ruhlmann at the 'Exposition Internationale des Arts Décoratifs et Industriels Modernes'. On the pediment section the decor consists of flower foliage and fountains.

302   Console table and mirror in wrought iron. By Nics Frères. The finishing is done in the martelé technique in order to give the wrought iron an iridescent surface texture in accordance with Art Deco taste. Approx. 1925–1930.

303   A 'Noblesse' console table, above which hangs a 'Transition' wall mirror with floral decor on pediment section, and two tall 'Orient' candlesticks with alabaster bases. Ensemble and sculpture by Edgar Brandt. Exhibited in 1926 at the 'Exhibition of French Decorative Arts at the Metropolitan Museum of Art, New York'.

304   Dressing table by Armand Albert Rateau (1883–1938). The circular mirror revolves and both sides can be used. It is lit by light bulbs set in three stylized daisy forms in the bronze frame. Designed for Jeanne Lanvin. 1920–22. The flower motif was chosen in allusion to Jeanne Lanvin's daughter, Marguerite. Exhibited in 1926 in the Metropolitan Museum of Art, New York. *Musée des Arts Décoratifs, Paris.*

305   Jeanne Lanvin's bathroom. By Armand Albert Rateau (1883–1938). Above the wash-hand basin hangs a round adjustable toilet mirror, the base of which is composed of two alternate pheasants in stylized form. 1920–22. *Musée des Arts Décoratifs. Paris.*

306   Living-room furniture. By Süe et Mare, Paris. The dressing table is in Macassar ebony with gilt frame. Exhibited in 1925 at the 'Exposition Internationale des Arts Décoratifs' in Paris.

307   Design of dressing table by Jacques Ruhlmann (1879–1933). The decor on the table top takes up the theme of the mirror's circular form. 1927. *Galerie du Luxembourg, Paris.*

308   Dressing table by Jacques Ruhlmann (1879–1933) after the design in Ill. 307. Made entirely of Macassar ebony. *Galerie du Luxembourg, Paris.*

309   Bedroom suite with oval mirror unit. By Maurice Dufrèsne (1878–1955). Palisander and dark-stained wood with mother-of-pearl ornamentation and bronze appliqués. Approx. 1920–23. *Musée des Arts Décoratifs, Paris. Acc. No. 45276.*

310   Dressing table with adjustable mirror with three sections. In chrome steel and mirror glass. By René Herbst. 1930. Commissioned by Princess Aga Khan. *Private collection Maria de Beyrie.*

311   Fireplace decor in old mirror glass. By Serge Roche. In front a small table also by Serge Roche. 1936–37. 2.10 × 1.40 m. *Serge Roche Collection.*

312   Design of console mirror. By Serge Roche. 1936–1937. Frame in red mirror glass. 1.50 × 1.20 m. *Serge Roche Collection.*

313   Round wall mirror. By Serge Roche. 1936–1937. The double-layer is made of mirror glass segments. 1936–37.

314   Octagonal mirror with inscribed decagonal star. By Serge Roche. Mirror glass frame. 0.95 × 0.80 m. 1936–37. *Serge Roche Collection.*

315   Sun-shaped mirror with diverging rays in mirror glass. Artist unknown. 1930–35.

316   Pentagonal mirror inscribed within two disjointed pentagonal frame sections. By Mario Andreü. In gilt wood, cellophane, and glazed paper. 1930–35.

Bibliography

FRANCE

Alciat, Livre d'emblèmes. 1536.
Ancienne Collection Jacques Doucet – Mobilier Art Deco, provenant du Studio Saint-James à Neuilly, Catalogue Hotel Drouot, 8 nov. 1972.
André Mare et la Compagnie des Arts Français (Süe et Mare). Catalogue Strasbourg 1971.
J. Baltrusaitis, Anamorphoses et perspectives curieuses. Paris 1955.
J. Barrelet, La verrerie en France. Paris 1953.
M. Battersby, The World of Art Nouveau. London 1968.
M. Battersby, The Decorative Twenties. London 1969.
M. Battersby, The Decorative Thirties. London 1971.
Bibliothèque Forney, L'encadrement-techniques et réalisations. Paris.
A. Blum, Histoire du costume, des modes aux XVIIe et XVIIIe siècles, 1928.
Bodin, De la Démonomanie des Sorciers. Paris 1580.
H. Bouilhet, Orfèvrerie française. 1910.
Bourgeois, Biscuit de Sèvres au XVIIIe siècle. Paris 1909.
J. Brinkmann, Die Ankäufe auf der Weltausstellung Paris 1900. Hamburg 1901.
Y. Brunhammer, 1925. Paris 1976.
Y. Brunhammer, Le Style 1925. Paris.
Cadres. Galerie Georges Petit, Paris, 1931, organisée par Serge Roche sous la présidence d'honneur de M. M. A. Pératé, conservateur en chef du musée de Versailles.
Cadres de Miroirs. Galerie André Arbus. Paris 1937.
E. Cases, L. Bernard, Le château de Versailles. 1910.
M. Chompré, Dictionnaire abrégé de la fable. Lyon 1782.
H. Clouzot, Le Style moderne dans la décoration moderne. Paris 1921.
H. Clouzot, La Ferronnerie Moderne. Paris, ca. 1925.
A. Cochin, Histoire de la manufacture des glaces de Saint-Gobain. 1865.
J. Compte, L'art à l'Exposition Universelle de 1900. Paris 1900.
R. Constantino, How to Know French Antiques. London 1963.
L. Deshairs, L'Art décoratif français 1918–1925. Paris 1925.
L. Deshairs, Intérieurs en couleurs. France. Paris 1926.
Diderot et d'Alembert, Encyclopédie. Paris 1751–1780.
Diversités Curieuses (manuscrit). Paris 1638.
P. D'Uckermann, L'Art dans la Vie Moderne. Paris 1937.
J. Dunand, J. Goulden, Catalogue d'Exposition, Galerie du Luxembourg. Paris 1973.
F. G. Dumas, L. de Fourcaud, Revue de l'Exposition Universelle de 1889. Paris 1889.
Emile-Bayard, L'Art appliqué français d'aujourd'hui. Paris, ca. 1925.
P. Fierens, La tristesse contemporaine. Paris 1924.
Fontaines et Vauxcelles, L'Art français de la révolution à nos jours, Paris.

– –, Encyclopédie des arts décoratifs et industriels modernes au XXe siècle. Paris 1926.
G. Fraipont, La fleur et ses applications décoratives. Paris.
E. Fremy, Histoire de la Manufacture royale des glaces de France. 1909.
E. Fry, Cubism, London, 1962.
Fuchs-Newberry, L'Exposition Internationale des Arts décoratifs Modernes. Darmstadt, 1902.
E. Gallé, Ecrits pour l'Art (1884–89). Paris 1908.
P. Garner, Émile Gallé. München, 1979. London 1976.
E. Grasset, La plante et ses applications ornamentales. Paris 1899.
Gravelot et Cochin, Iconologie ou traité des Allégories ou emblèmes. Paris 1791.
R. H. Guerrand, L'Art Nouveau en Europe. Paris 1967.
J. Guiffret, Inventaire général du mobilier de la couronne. 1885.
P. Guilmard, Les maîtres ornemanistes. Paris 1880.
H. Guimard, L'Art dans l'habitation moderne. Le Castel Béranger. Paris 1898.
H. Havard, Dictionnaire de l'ameublement. Paris 1887–1890.
R. Herbst, 25 Années Union des Artistes Modernes. Paris 1955.
B. Hillier, Art Deco. New York 1969.
B. Hillier, The World of Art Deco. London 1971.
F. L. Hinckley, A Directory of Antique French Furniture, 1735–1800. New York 1967.
G. Hoentschel, Le Pavillon de l'Union Centrale des Arts Décoratifs à l'Exposition Universelle de 1900. Paris 1900.
H. Hoffmann, Intérieurs Modernes de tous les Pays. Paris 1930.
R. Huyghe, Dialogue avec le visible. Paris 1955.
G. Janneau et P. Devinoy, Le meuble léger en France. Paris 1952.
P. Juyot, Louis Majorelle-Artiste Décorateur, maître-ébéniste. Nancy 1926.
R. Koechlin, Histoire des ivoires gothiques français. Paris 1924.
E. Langlois, Le Roman de la Rose. Paris 1922.
Le Corbusier, Towards a New Architecture. London 1927.
Ph. Leroux, Dictionnaire comique, satirique et burlesque, libre et proverbial. 1735.
J. Leurechin, Récréations mathématiques. Bar-le-Duc 1623.
Maze Sencier, Le livre des Collectionneurs. Paris 1885.
R. Menard, La Mythologie. Paris 1880.
Miroirs. Galerie Serge Roche, Paris, 1934, organisée sous la présidence d'honneur de M. François Carnot, Président de l'Union Centrale des Arts Décoratifs.
G. Mourey, Histoire générale de l'art français de la Révolution à nos jours. L'Art Décoratif. Paris 1925.
J. F. Niceron, La perspective curieuse. Paris 1638.
–, Nouvelles récréations physiques et mathématiques. Paris 1759.
P. Olmer, Le Mobilier Français d'Aujourd'hui (1910–1925). Paris 1926.

P. Olmer, La Renaissance du Mobilier Français. Paris 1927.
G. De Nolhac. La resurrection de Versailles. Paris 1937.
C. Paradin, Dévises héroiques. Lyon 1557.
J. Pena, Optique et catoptrique d'Euclide. Paris 1557.
N. Pevsner, Pioneers of Modern Design: From William Morris to Walter Gropius. London 1936, 1977.
P. Poiret, En Habillant l'Époque. Paris 1930.
G. Quenioux, Les Arts Décoratifs Modernes. Paris 1925.
M. Rheims, L'Art 1900. Paris 1965.
M. Rochas, Vingt-Cinq Ans d'Élégance à Paris. Paris 1951.
S. Roche, Cadres français et étrangers du XVe au XVIIIe siècle. 1931.
S. Roche et P. Devinoy, Miroirs – Galeries et Cabinets de glaces. Paris 1954.
L. Rousselet, L'Exposition Universelle de 1889. Paris 1889.
E.-J. Ruhlmann, Exposition Retrospective, Musée des Arts Décoratifs. Paris 1934.
R. Schmutzler, Art Nouveau. London 1964.
J. Vanuxem, Emblèmes et devises vers 1660–1680. (Bulletin de la Société de l'histoire de l'art français). 1934.
M. P. Verneuil, L'Animal dans la Décoration. Paris 1898.
Viollet-Le-Duc, Dictionnaire raisonné du Mobilier français. Paris 1858.
E. de Vogue, Remarques sur L'Exposition de 1889. Paris 1889.
J. Wilhem, La Vie à Paris sous le Second Empire et la IIIe Republique. 1947.

BELGIUM

Art Nouveau Belgium-France, Exhibition Catalogue, Institute for the Arts, Rice University. Houston 1976.
F. Borst, Bruxelles 1900. Bruxelles 1974.
S. Henrion-Giele, Musée Horta. Bruxelles 1972.
H. Hoffmann, Intérieurs Modernes de Tous les Pays. Paris 1930.
H. F. Lenning, The Art Nouveau. Den Haag 1951.
Pionniers Du XXe Siecle. Guimard, Horta, Van De Velde. Catalogue d'exposition. Musée des Arts Décoratifs. Paris 1971.
H. Van De Velde, Catalogue d'exposition, l'Ecuyer. Bruxelles 1907.
H. Van De Velde, Geschichte meines Lebens. München 1962.
H. Van De Velde, Zum neuen Stil. München 1955.

HOLLAND

C. H. De Jonge, Holländische Möbel- und Raumkunst. Stuttgart 1922.
F. Leidelmeijer, D. Van Der Cingel, Art Nouveau an Art Déco in Nederland. Amsterdam 1983.
H. L. C. Jaffe, De Stijl. London 1970.
H. F. Lenning, The Art Nouveau. Den Haag 1951.

P. OVERY, De Stijl. London, 1969.

P. SCHEUK, Das Buch der Zahlen und verschlungenen Embleme. Holland, 17. Jh.

GERMANY

K. P. ARNOLD, Gestaltete Form in Vergangenheit und Gegenwart; Möbel aus Hellerau. Museum für Kunsthandwerk. Dresden 1973.

M. BALFOUR, The Kaiser and his Times. London 1964.

A. BANGERT, Jugendstil, Art Deco: Möbel und Interieur. München 1980.

K. BAUCH, H. SELING, Jugendstil. Der Weg ins 20. Jahrhundert. München 1959.

BAUHAUS, Royal Academy. London 1973.

H. BAYER, W. Gropius, Ilse Gropius, Bauhaus 1919–28, Museum of Modern Art, New York 1938, 1975.

W. BEHRENDT, Der Kampf um den Stil in Kunstgewerbe und Architektur. Berlin 1920.

G. BOTT, Jugendstil in Darmstadt um 1900. Darmstadt 1962.

G. BOTT, Jugendstil. Kataloge des Hessischen Landesmuseums Nr. 1. Darmstadt 1973.

L. BURCKHARDT, Werkbund Germania, Austria, Svizzera. Venezia 1977.

I. CREMONA, Die Zeit des Jugendstils. München–Wien 1966.

P. DETLESSEN, Projet d'un château destiné au roi de Bavière, par Paulus Decker, architecte. Augsburg 1711.

C. GRIMM, Alte Bilderrahmen. München 1978.

R. GRAUL, Die Krisis im Kunstgewerbe. Leipzig 1901.

C. GURLITT, Das Barock- und Rococo-Ornament Deutschlands. Berlin 1889.

G. F. HARTLAUB, Zauber des Spiegels. München 1961.

C. G. HEISE, Die Kunst des 20. Jahrhunderts. Malerei, Plastik, Raum, Gerät. München 1957.

J. HERMAND, Jugendstil. Forschungsbericht 1918–1964. Stuttgart 1965.

W. HOFMANN, Von der Nachahmung zur Erfindung der Wirklichkeit. Die schöpferische Befreiung der Kunst. 1890 bis 1917. Köln 1970.

H. H. HOFSTÄTTER, Symbolismus und die Kunst der Jahrhundertwende. Köln 1965, 1973.

JAHRBUCH DES DEUTSCHEN WERKBUNDES. Jena 1912–14. München 1913.

L. KLEINER, Josef Hoffmann. Berlin 1927.

H. KREISEL, Deutsche Spiegelkabinette. Darmstadt 1955.

KUNSTHANDWERK UND INDUSTRIEFORM DES 19. UND 20. JAHRHUNDERTS. Staatl. Kunstsammlungen. Dresden 1976.

J. LESSING, Vorbilder, Hefte aus dem kgl. Kunstgewerbemuseum. Berlin 1889–1905.

F. LÖFFLER, E. BERTONATI, Dresdner Sezession 1919–1925. Galleria del Levante. München 1977.

J. MEIER-GRAEFE, Die Weltausstellung in Paris 1900. Berlin 1907.

H. MUTHESIUS, *Kunst und Maschine*, in: Dekorative Kunst, Band 9, 1902.

H. OBRIST, Zweckmäßig oder Phantasievoll. München 1901.

M. OSBORN, Die Kunst des „Rokoko". Berlin 1920.

SCHMIDT, Das Glas. Berlin 1912.

H. SCHMITZ, Das Möbelwerk. Tübingen, 1963.

R. SCHMUTZLER, Art Nouveau – Jugendstil, Stuttgart 1962.

R. SEDLMAIER, R. PFISTER, Die Fürstbischöfliche Residenz zu Würzburg. München 1923.

K. J. SEMBACH, Stil 1930. Tübingen 1971, 1984.

H. SPIELMANN, Der Jugendstil in Hamburg. Hamburg 1965.

G. STERNER, Jugendstil. Köln 1975.

TENDENZEN DER ZWANZIGER JAHRE, 15. Europäische Kunstausstellung. Berlin 1977.

G. B. V. HARTMANN, W. FISCHER, Zwischen Kunst und Industrie des Deutschen Werkbunds. Die Neue Sammlung. München 1975.

H. VAN DE VELDE, Geschichte meines Lebens. München 1962.

H. M. WINGLER, The Bauhaus. Boston 1969.

AUSTRIA

V. BEHAL, Möbel des Jugendstils. München 1981.

H. BAHR, Sezession. Wien 1900.

R. BÖHMER, Spiegelbräun im Zeitalter Ludwigs XIV., Wien 1946.

M. EISLER, Österreichische Werkkultur. Wien 1916.

J. HOFFMANN, Einfache Möbel. Das Interieur. Wien 1901.

C. HOLME, The Art Revival in Austria. London 1906.

L. KLEINER, Josef Hoffmann. Berlin 1927.

W. MRAZEK, Die Wiener Werkstätte. Modernes Kunsthandwerk von 1903–1932. Österreichisches Kunstgewerbemuseum. Wien 1967.

ÖSTERREICH AUF DER WELTAUSSTELLUNG PARIS 1900. Wien 1900.

N. POWELL, The Sacred Spring. The Arts in Vienna 1898–1918. London 1974.

R. SCHMIDT, Das Wiener Künstlerhaus. Wien 1964.

E. F. SEKLER, „Mackintosh and Vienna", repr. in: The Anti-Rationalist. London 1973.

P. VERGO, Art in Vienna, 1898–1918. London 1975.

G. VERONESI, Josef Hoffmann. Milano 1956.

VIENNA SECESSION, ART NOUVEAU TO 1970. Royal Academy, London 1971.

O. WAGNER, Moderne Architektur. Wien 1895.

SWITZERLAND

A. CHAPUIS, E. GELIS, Le monde des automates. Paris 1928.

LE CORBUSIER, Toward a New Architecture. Paris 1923. London 1927.

LE CORBUSIER, Le Corbusier et Pierre Jeanneret: Oeuvres Complètes de 1910–29. Zürich 1948.

ITALY

L. B. ALBERTI, Della Pittura. 1435.

E. BAIRATI, L'Italia Liberty. Arredamento e arti decorative. Firenze 1964.

R. BOSSAGLIA, Il Liberty in Italia. Milano 1968.

R. BOSSAGLIA, Il ‚Deco' Italiano. Fisionomia dello Stile 1925 in Italia. Milano 1975.

V. BROSIO, Lo Stile Liberty in Italia. Milano 1967.

C. CAMILLO, G. PORSO, Livre d'emblèmes. Padova 1586.

L. DA VINCI, De la Science. 1508.

J. B. DELLA PORTA, Magia Naturalis. Napoli 1589.

G. G. GÖRLICH, Il Mobile Veneziano del 1700. Milano 1956.

A. KIRCHER, Ars Magna Lucis. Roma 1646.

LACCHE VENEZIANE DEL SETTECENTO. Palazzo Rezzonico. Venezia 1938.

G. MARAZZONI, Mobilier vénitien du XVIIe siècle. Milano 1927.

G. PICCINI, Nouveau livre des cabinets de glace et miroirs inventés par le sieur Giovanni Piccini, architecte ordinaire de S.A.S. le duc de Modène. Paris 1685.

A. PICA, Storia della Triennale 1918–1957. Milano 1957.

TUMINELLI, BESTATTI, Miroirs vénitiens. Milano 1950.

G. VASARI, La vie des plus célèbres peintres, sculpteurs et architectes (1512–1574). Firenze 1905.

SPAIN

J. E. CIRLOT, El Estilo del Siglo XX. Barcelona 1952.

G. R. COLLINS, Antonio Gaudi. New York 1960.

A. C. PELLICER, El arte modernista catalan. Barcelona 1951.

A. C. PELLICER, 1900 en Barcelona. Barcelona 1967.

J. PRATS VALLEZ, Gaudi. Barcelona 1958.

G. STERNER, Antoni Gaudi. Köln 1979.

J. J. SWEENEY, L. S. SERT, Antoni Gaudi. London 1960.

SCANDINAVIA

J. BOULTON SMITH, The Golden Age of Finnish Art (Art Nouveau). Helsinki 1976.

E. STAVENOW-HIDEMARK, Svensk Jugend. Stockholm, Nordiska Museet 1964.

UNITED KINGDOM

A. ADBURGHAM et al, Liberty's 1875–1975. Catalogue of an exhibition at the Victoria and Albert Museum. London 1975.

J. ALLWOOD, The Great Exhibitions. London 1977.

I. ANSCOMBE, CH. GERE, Arts and Crafts in Britain and America. London 1978.

C. ASHBEE, A Short History of the Guild and School of Handicraft. London 1890.

E. ASLIN, The Aesthetic Mouvement, Prelude to Art Nouveau. London 1969.

R. BANHAM, Theory and Design in the First Machine Age. London 1960.

M. BATTERSBY, The Decorative Twenties. London 1969.

M. BATTERSBY, The Decoratice Thirties. London 1971.

A. BOE, From Gothic Revival to Functional Form. Oslo 1957.

O. BRACKETT, Englische Möbel. Berlin 1927.

H. CESCINSKY, English Furniture from Gothic to Sheraton. New York 1968.

T. CHIPPENDALE, The Gentleman and Cabinet-Maker's Director. New York 1966.

P. COLLINS, Changing Ideals in Modern Architecture. 1750–1950. London 1967.

W. CRANE, Line and Form. London 1900.

C. DRESSER, The Art of Decorative Design. London 1882.

R. EDWARDS, L. G. G. RAMSEY, The Connoisseur's Complete Period Guides to the Houses, Decoration, Furnishing and Chattels of the Classic Periods. New York 1968.

R. EDWARDS, The Shorter Dictionary of English Furniture from the Middle Ages to the Late Georgian Period. London 1964.

E. V. Gillon jr., Decorative Frames and Borders. New York 1973.

A. Heal, The London Furniture Makers, from the Restoration to the Victorian Era, 1660–1840. London 1960.

P. Henderson, William Morris, his Life, Work and Friends. London 1967.

G. Hepplewhite, The Cabinetmaker and Upholsterer's Guide. New York 1969.

T. Hope, Household Furniture and Interior Decoration. Classic Style Book of the Regency Period. New York 1971.

T. Howarth, Charles Rennie Mackintosh and the Modern Movement. London 1952.

Ince & Mayhew, The Universal System of Household Furniture. London 1960.

O. Jones, Grammar of Ornament. London 1856.

W. R. Lethaby, Form in Civilisation. London 1922.

F. Mac Carthy, All Things Bright and Beautiful. Design in Britain, 1830 to Today. London 1972.

J. W. Mackail, The Life of William Morris. London 1899.

G. Naylor, The Arts and Crafts Movement. London 1971.

W. Nutting, Furniture Treasury. New York 1928.

N. Pevsner, An Enquiry into Industrial Art in England. London 1937.

–, Pioneers of Modern Design from William Morris to Walter Gropius. New York 1949.

–, Charles Rennie Mackintosh. Milano 1950.

–, The Sources of Modern Architecture and Design. London 1968.

–, Studies in Art, Architecture and Design. London 1968.

M. Praz, An Illustrated History of Interior Decoration from Pompei to Art Nouveau. London 1982.

M. B. Schiffer, The Mirror Book. Exton 1983.

B. Schweig, Mirrors – A Guide to the Manufacture of Mirrors and Reflecting Surfaces. London 1973.

R. W. Symonds, Furniture Making in Seventeenth and Eighteenth Century England. An Outline for Collectors. London 1955.

The Studio Yearbooks of Decorative Art. London 1906–1930.

The Year Book of the Design in Industries Association. London 1922–1930.

D. Todd, R. Mortimer, The New Interior Decoration. London 1929.

P. Ward-Jackson, English Furniture Designs of the Eighteens Century. Victoria and Albert Museum. London 1959.

G. Wills, English Looking Glasses: a study of the glass, frames and makers. 1670–1820. London 1965.

U.S.A.

E. B. Bates, J. L. Fairbanks, American Furniture, 1620 to the Present. New York 1981.

E. H. Bjerkoe, The Cabinetmakers of America. Exton 1978.

D. J. Bush, The Streamlined Decade. New York 1975.

R. J. Clarke, The Arts and Crafts Movement in America 1876–1916. Exhibition Catalogue. Princeton 1972.

H. Comstock, The Looking Glass in America, 1700–1825. New York 1968.

H. Comstock, American Furniture. 17th, 18th and 19th Century Styles. New York 1962.

T. A. Cook, The Curves of Life. New York 1914.

S. Giedion, Mechanization takes Command. New York 1948.

H.-R. Hitchcock, Architecture: Nineteenth and Twentieth Centuries, London 1958.

G. Holme, Industrial Design and the Future. London, New York 1934.

R. Koch, Louis C. Tiffany, Rebel in Glass. New York 1974.

K. Morrison, McClinton, Art Deco – A guide for Collectors. New York 1973.

W. Nutting, Furniture Treasury. New York 1928.

B. Ring, „Checklist of looking-glass and frame makers and merchants known by their labels." In: The Magazine Antiques, May 1981.

H. Schaeffer, The Roots of Modern Design. London 1970.

M. B. Schiffer, The Mirror Book. Exton 1983.

B. Schweig, Mirrors, A Guide to the Manufacture of Mirrors and Reflecting Surfaces. London 1973.

P. Strickland, „Documented Philadelphia looking-glass Manufacturers, circa 1800–1850". In: The Magazine Antiques. April 1976.

The Brooklyn Museum

RUSSIA

Die Kunstismen in Russland, 1907–1930. Katalog Galerie Gmurzynska. Köln 1977.

Filiminoff, Inventaire du Palais des Armures. Moscou 1884–1893.

Fabergé, 1846–1920, Exhibition Catalogue, Victoria and Albert Museum. London 1977.

Foelkerzam, Inventaire de l'argenterie des Palais Impériaux 1907.

C. Gray, The Great Experience, Russian Art 1863–1922. London 1962.

Loukomski, Anciens Palais Impériaux Russes. Petrograd 1916.

Loukomski, Tsarköe Selo. München 1923.

E. H. Minns, Scythians and Greeks. Cambridge 1923.

N. Peakock, „The New Movement in Russian Decorative Art", The Studio, vol. 22, 1901.

A. Pouchkine, Contes. Paris 1925.

Tolstoi, Kondakoff, Antiquités Russes (Monuments de l'art, vol. II). Petersbourg 1889.

JAPAN

Fujita, Poèmes japonais receuillis et illustrés. 1922.

CHINA

S. Umeharo, Étude sur le miroir antérieur à la dynastie des „Han". Academy of oriental culture, Kyoto Institute. 1935.

Cent Quatrains des „Tang", traduits par Lo Tan Kang. Neuchâtel 1947.

W. Cohn, Peinture chinoise. Paris 1948.

Picture acknowledgments

Bayerisches Nationalmuseum München: 115, 116, 282. – Bayerische Verwaltung der staatlichen Schlösser, Gärten und Seen. Schloß Nymphenburg: 148, 149, 152, 153, 159, 164, 165. – Bildarchiv Preußischer Kulturbesitz: IV, IX. – The Brooklyn Museum: 199, 203. – A. Chadefaux, Agence TOP: XVI. – Atelier Dager, Montrouge: 98. – R. Descharnes, Paris: 286. – Editions Illustration, Paris: 296, 297, 298, 299, 300, 301, 305, 307. – Felipe Ferré, Paris: XIV. – Françoise Foliot: 285. – Studio Grünke, Hamburg: 277. – Photo Gundermann, Würzburg: 154. – Jaroslav Guth, Bavaria-Verlag Bildagentur: VI. – Wolfdietrich Hassfurther, Wien: 293, 294, 295. – Manfred Heinrich, Reutlingen: 130, XV. – Dr. Hellmut Hell, Reutlingen: 29, 30, 165. – Erik Hesmerg: 279. – Frank Horvat, Agence Rapho Paris: 32. –

P. Jahan, Paris: XI, XIII, 215, 315. – Galerie Jacques Kugel, Paris: V, VII. – Kunstgewerbemuseum. Staatliche Museen Preußischer Kulturbesitz, Berlin (West): 270. – Mathildenhöhe Darmstadt: 283, 284. – Mittelrheinisches Landesmuseum Mainz: 278. – Musée des Arts Décoratifs, Paris: 102. – Musée des Arts Décoratifs, Paris. Photo L. Sully-Jaulmes: 273, 274, 275, 309. – Museum für Kunst und Gewerbe, Hamburg: 15, 276, 287. – Museum für Ostasiatische Kunst, Köln: I. – The Museum of Modern Art, New York. Gift of Joseph H. Heil: 271. – The Metropolitan Museum of Art: 27 (Gift of G. Leonberger Davis, 1967. No. 67.146.2), 28 (Fletcher Fund, 1972. No. 1972.24). – Österreichisches Museum für Angewandte Kunst, Wien: 288, 289, 290, 291, 292. – Marlen Perez, Museum Bellerive, Zürich: 272, 281. –

Réunion des Musées Nationaux: II (Cliché no. 78 E 924), III (Cliché no. D 64 E 76), XII (Cliché no. 82 E 525), 49 (Cliché no. 80 CN 12 277), 76 (Cliché no. 67 EN 1463). – Rheinisches Bildarchiv, Köln: 19. – Rijksmuseum Stichting Amsterdam: 114. – Serge Roche: 22, 66, 72, 75, 90, 98, 110, 111, 121, 122, 125, 126, 128, 180, 181, 182, 183, 184, 185, 190, 193, 195, 213, 221, 229, 232, 233, 254, 256, 311, 312, 316. – E. Schmachtenberger, Bavaria-Verlag Bildagentur: VIII. – Sotheby's Belgravia: 280, 308. – Staatliches Museum für Völkerkunde, München: 20. – Thames & Hudson Ltd., London: 302, 303, 304, 306, 310. – Victoria and Albert Museum, London: 175. – Verlag Ernst Wasmuth, Tübingen: 169, 170, 171, 176, 177, 178, 187, 188.

1.   The five reflections of the 60 degrees angle.

1–4.   Catoptrical studies.

2, 3

2

4.   Only one thing in the hexagonal space.

 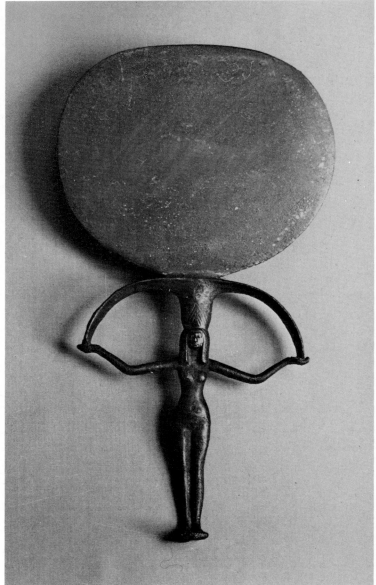

5.   Egypt. Bronze hand-mirror. Wood handle. About 1400 B.C.   6.   Egypt. Bronze hand-mirror. About 1400 B.C.

7. Etruscan hand-mirror. Bronze. 4th c. B.C.   8. Greco-roman hand-mirror. Silver. 2nd c. A.D.

9.   Greece. Bronze mirror. 4th c. B.C.

10.   Greece. Bronze mirror. 4th c. B.C.

6

11. Greece. Bronze mirror with pedestal.
5th c. B.C.

13. Greece. Bronze mirror with pedestal.
Beginning of 5th c. B.C.

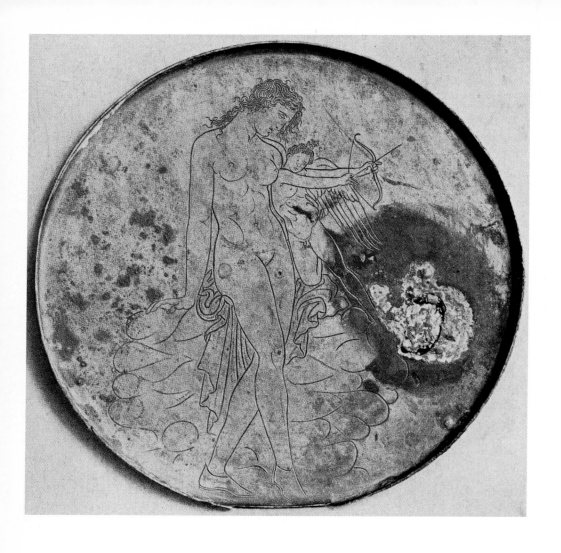

14. South Italy. Bronze folding mirror. About 350 B.C.

15.   Etruscan hand-mirror. Bronze. 3rd c. B.C.

16.   Etruscan hand-mirror. Bronze. 4th c. B.C.

◁ 18.   China. Bronze mirrors. 2nd c. A.D.   19.   Japan. Bronze mirror. Kamakura period. 13th c.

13

20. Yombe, Zaire. Magical wooden statuette. "Nduda".

21. Coptic Egypt. Wooden comb inlaid with broken glass.

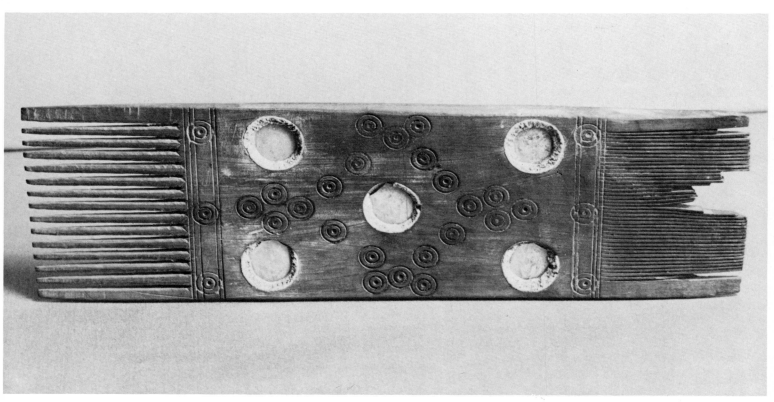

22.   Coptic Egypt. The siren tapestry.

23.   Egypt. Plate of tinned glass in a fragment of limestone.

24.   Arabian Egypt. Bronze mirror. 14th c.

25, 26.   Peria. Mirror framed in jade inlaid
with ruby. Beginning of 18th c.

28. Persia. Hand-mirror framed in burnished
steel. 17th c.

29. Persia.
Golestan Palace, Teheran.
Staircase to throne room.
Early 19th c.

30.   Persia. Golestan Palace, Teheran. Peacock Throne. Early 19th c.

31. Persia. Mirror framed in polychrome wood. End of 18th c.

32.   Pakistan. Reflected image of the bride.

33.   Pre-Columbian America. Iron pyrites mirror lying on mirror of polished obsidian.

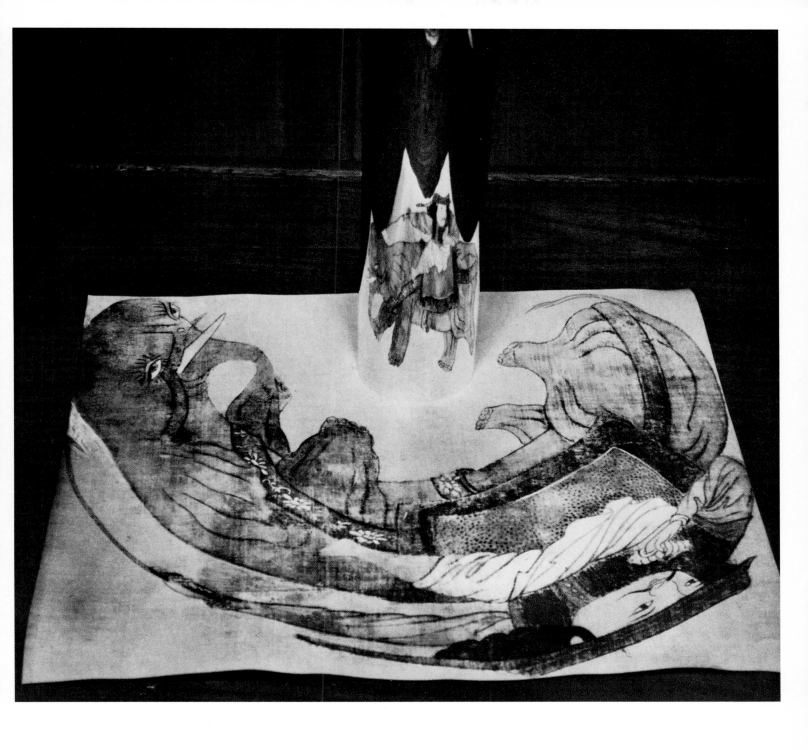

34. China. Catoptrical anamorphosis. 17th c.

35

36

37

38

35, 36. Ivory mirror case. First half of 14th c.   37, 38. Ivory mirror case. First half of 14th c.

26

39. Carved ivory mirror case. 14th c.

40.   Lid of ivory mirror case. First half of 16th c.

41.   Carved wood comb and mirror. 16th c.

42.   Hand-mirror. Carved ivory. 16th c.

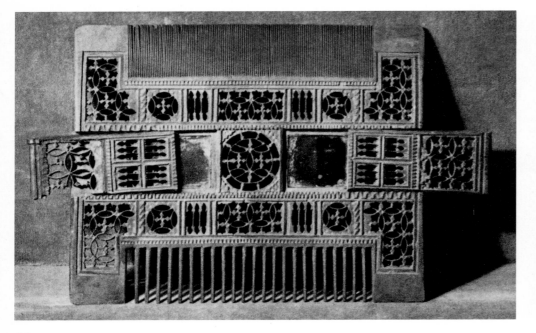

44, 45, 46.   Hand-mirrors. Sketches from Delaune, called Stephanus. 16th c.

47. Hand-mirror. Iron with silver inlay. 16th c.

48.   Walnut mirror case with a sliding panel.
16th c.

49.   Hand-mirror. Iron with silver inlay.
16th c.

50, 51. Pocket mirrors. 16th c.

52. Detail of an oval mirror.
Walnut. Louis XIII.

53, 54. Convex mirrors. Louis XIII. ▷

56.   Detail of the preceding mirror. Three Muses.

◁ 55.   Mirror framed in gilt wood. Apollo and the Muses. 17th c.

57, 58.　Mirror framed in gilt wood with pediment and mirror panels. Louis XIV.

61. Mirror framed in
gilt wood and mirror
panels. Regence.

62.   Mirror framed in gilt wood. Louis XIV.

63. France. Louis XIV mirror with pediment in gilt wood and red lacquer. Early 18th c.

64. Mirror with pediment. Gilt wood glass painted red and gilded on reverse. Louis XIV. ▷

67, 68.   Hand-mirror framed in gilt bronze.
Regence.

68

69. Toilet-mirror with support. Bronze and tortoise-shell. Louis XIV.

70. Toilet-mirror with support. Bronze and tortoise-shell. Louis XIV.

71.   Overmantel-mirror. Gilt wood. Louis XV.

72.   Toilet-mirror framed in silver. 18th c.

73. Mirror framed in bisque (Sèvres) from the Comtesse du Nord's dressing-table.

74. Pier. Table mirror. Gilt wood. Louis XV.

76.   Pier-glass. First half of 18th c.   ▷

77.　Mirror with pediment. Gilt wood. Louis XVI.

78.   Mirror with pediment. Natural wood. Louis XVI.

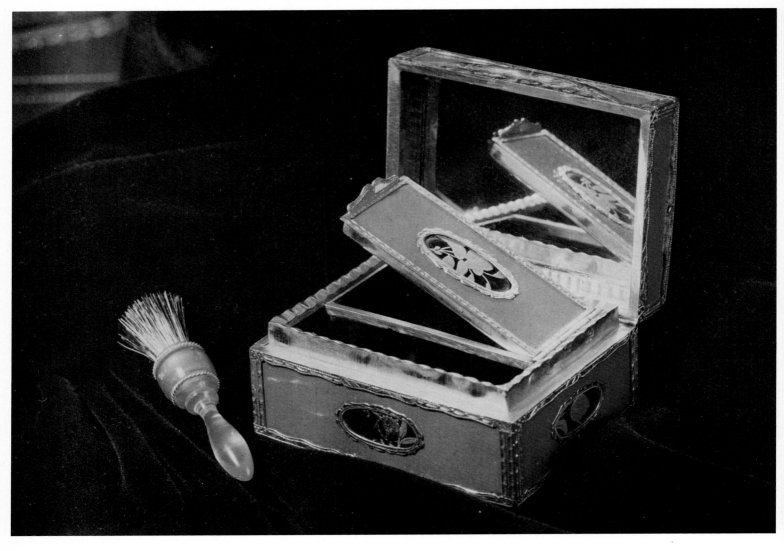

79. Marquise de Pompadour's patch-box.

80, 81. Madame de Balbi's small leather case.
End of 18th c.

82, 83. Small leather dressing-case. 18th c.

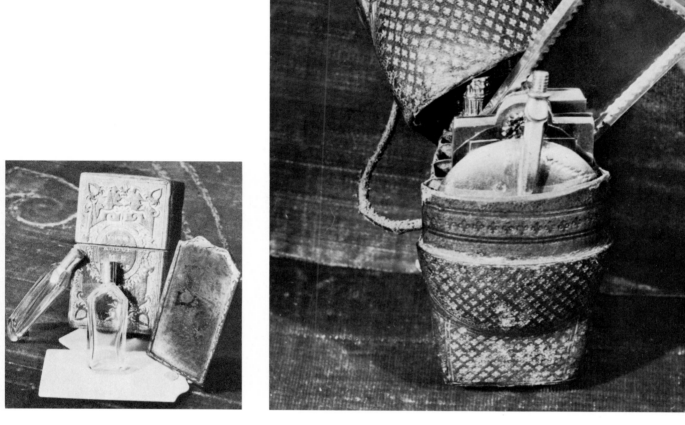

84. Small leather cutlery-case. 18th c.

85. Dressing-table of Queen Marie-Antoinette in prison.

86. Mirrors from Queen Marie-Antoinette's dressing-case.

87. Silver travelling-case. End of 18th c. ▷

88. Oval mirror framed in iron. End of 18th c.

89. Sketch of a silver plate dressing-table mirror. Louis XVI.

90. Trophy-shaped
mirror. End of 18th c.

91. Microscope with mirror. Gilt bronze and shagreen. By Magny. 1750.

92. Centre-piece. Glass and gilt wood. 17th c.

93. King Jérôme's toilet-case. Empire style.

94. Dressing-table in mahogany and bronze. Empire style.

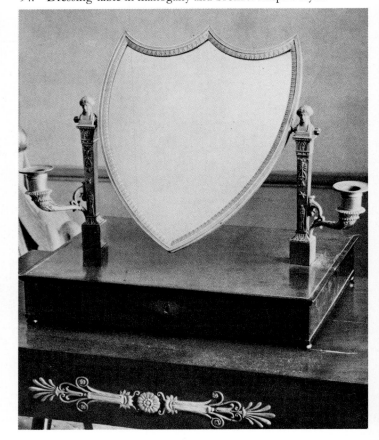

95. Mirror "à la Montgolfière". Gilt wood.
End of 18th c.

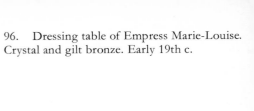

96. Dressing table of Empress Marie-Louise. Crystal and gilt bronze. Early 19th c.

97. Cheval-glass in mahogany and bronze. ▷ Empire.

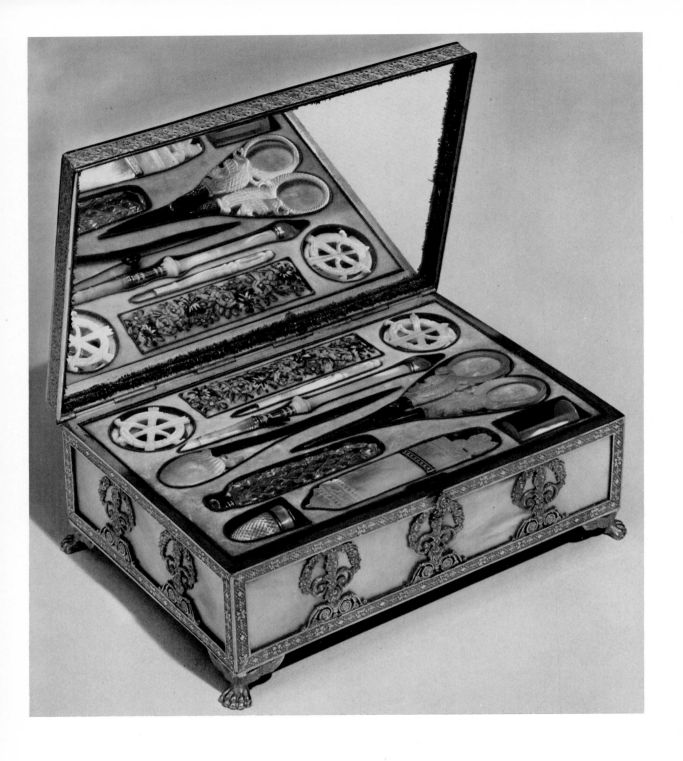

98.   Work-box. Mother of pearl and bronze. About 1820.

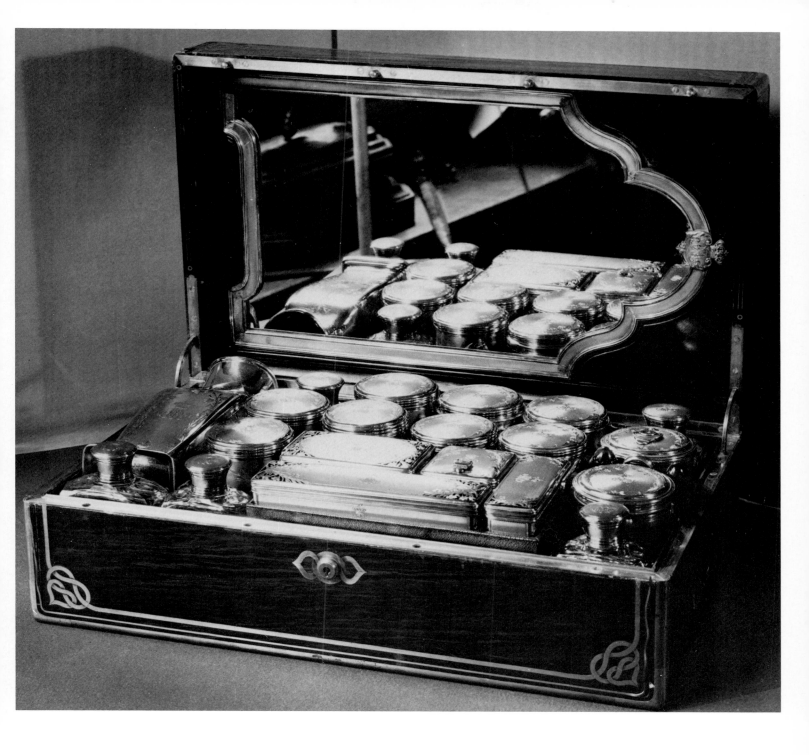

99. Queen Maria-Amelia's toilet-case. Beginning of 19th c.

100. Silver toilet-case. Beginning of 19th c.

101.   Toilet-case belonging to the emperor of Brazil. Beginning of 19th c.

102.   Mirror framed in bronze. "Troubadour" style. 19th c.

103.   Baccarat mirror framed in enamel and blue and white glass. End of 19th c.

105. Palace of Versailles. "War Drawing-Room". Louis XIV.

74

106.   Palace of Versailles. The hall of mirrors. Louis XIV.

107.   Palace of Versailles. The hall of mirrors. Louis XIV.

108.   Beauharnais Mansion. Bath-room. Empire style.

109.   Overmantel-mirror. Painted and gilt wood. End of 17th c.

110, 111.   Toilet-mirrors framed in gilt wood. Lutma style. 17th c.

112. Mirror framed in gilt bronze and steel. Flemish. Beginning of 18th c.

115. Germany. Mirror framed in carved wood. With symbolic statuettes. 16th c. ▷

113. Mirror framed in gilt wood decorated with the signs of the zodiac. 17th c.

114. Mirror framed in Delft faience. 17th c.

81

◁ 116.   Justice. Detail of mirror 115.

117, 118.   Standing mirror. Ivory and vermeil. End of 16th c.

119, 120.   Mirror framed in gilt wood. End of 18th c.

120

121.   Mirror framed in metal. 16th c.

122.   Mirror framed in Dresden china. 18th c.

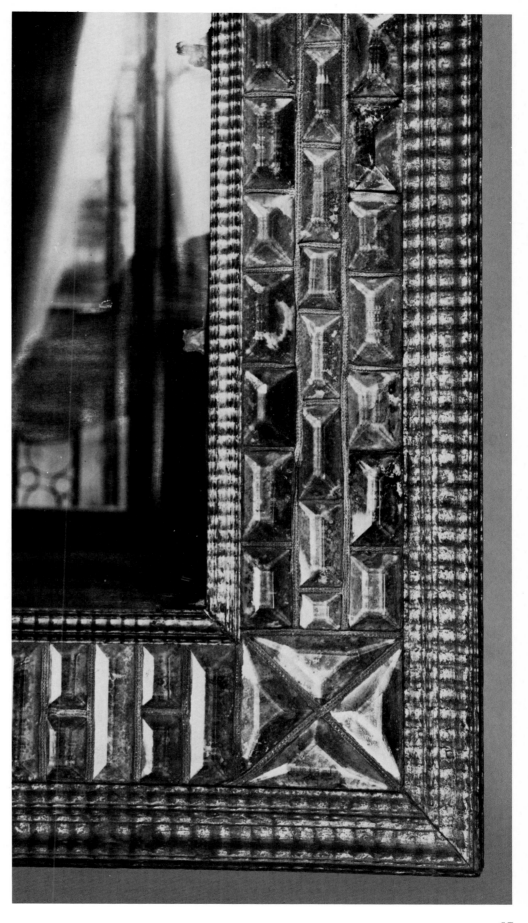

123, 124.   Mirror with frame in gilt wood
and Bohemian glass. Beginning of 17th c.

125.   Austria. Mirror with pediment. Gilt wood and engraved glass. 18th c.

126.   Hungary. Mirror with pediment. Gilt wood and engraved glass. 18th c.

127.   Mirror framed in polychrome faience. 18th c.   ▷

129. Austria. Engraved mirror pediment. Rococo style 18th c.

130. Mirror with pediment in engraved crystal glass. 19th c.

131.   Augsburg. Mirror in silver, electrum, tortoise-shell and engraved mirror glass. 1699.

132.   Sketch of a mirror room by Paulus Decker. 1711.

133.   Palace of Charlottenburg. China room. Beginning of 18th c.

135

135–138.   Palace of Pommersfelden. Mirror room. Beginning of 18th c.

137

137, 138.   Palace of Pommersfelden. Mirror room. Beginning of 18th c.

139

139–142.   Rastatt. Residence of "La Favorite". The mirror room. Beginning of 18th c.

140

141, 142.   Rastatt. Residence of "La Favorite". The mirror room. Beginning of 18th c.

143, 145.   Residence of "La Favorite". Reception-room. Beginning of 18th c.

144.   Residence of "La Favorite". The mirror room. Beginning of 18th c.

146, 147.   Rastatt. Residence of "La Favorite".
The Florentine room. Beginning of 18th c.

148, 149.   Munich. Nymphenburg Palace, Residence of Amalienburg. Mirror room. By François Cuvilliés. 1739.

150, 151.   Munich, Nymphenburg Palace, Residence of Amalienburg. The mirror room. Beginning of 18th c.

152.   Munich, Residence. State bedroom. After a design by François Cuvilliés. 1731–33.

153.   Munich, Residence. Mirror room. After a design by François Cuvilliés. 1731–33.

154. Würzburg, Residence. Mirror room.
After a design by Johann Wolfgang von der
Auvera. 1742–45.

155–158. Palace of Ludwigsburg. Mirror room. Beginning of 18th c.

157, 158.   Palace of Ludwigsburg. Mirror room. Beginning of 18th c.

159, 160.   Ansbach, Residence. Mirror room. First third of 18th c.

161, 162.   Bayreuth. Palace of the Hermitage. Mirror decorations. Middle of 18th c.

163, 164. Bayreuth. Mirror room of the new palace. Middle of 18th c.

166.   Andechs. Cupola of the chapel. Middle of 18th c.

◁ 165.   Zwiefalten. Cupola of the church. Middle of 18th c.

167, 168.   Mirror with pediment framed in
blue and white glass. End of 17th c.

170.   Mirror with sconces. Late 17th
and early 18th c.   ▷

169. Mirror frame with marquetry. Late 17th c.

168

171.   Gilt mirror frame. Queen Anne period. Early 18th c.

172, 173.   Dressing-table mirror with embroidered decoration. 17th c.

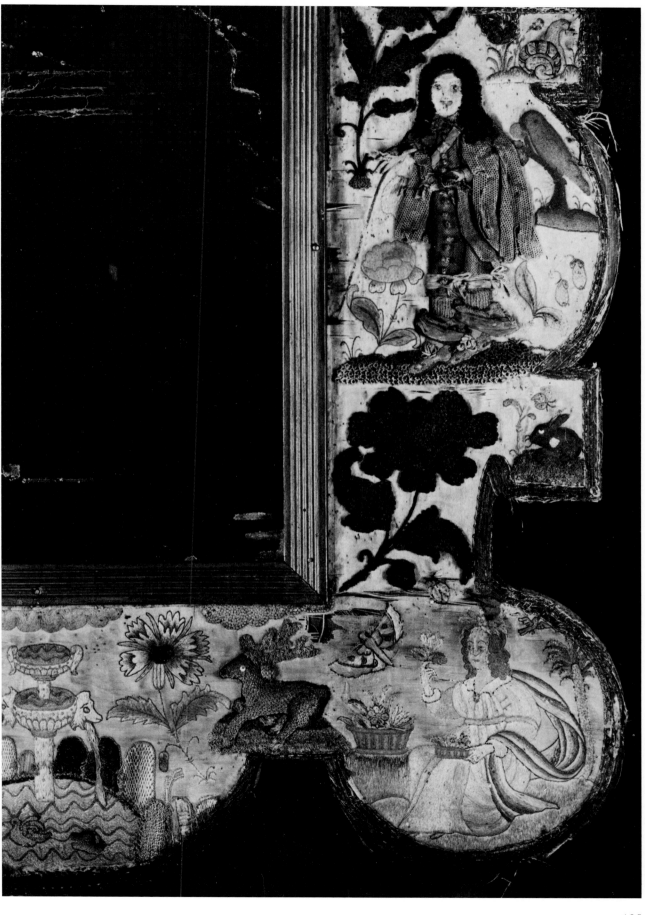

174.   Dressing-table mirror. Framed in silver plated. 18th c.

175.   Gilt wood mirror. Grinling-Gibbons style. End of 17th c.

176.   Gilt wood mirror. Grinling-Gibbons style. End of 17th c.

177.   Rectangular overmantel
mirror. King William III period.
Late 17th c.

178.   Mirror framed in gilt wood. Chippendale style. About 1755.

179.   Mirror framed in red and gilt lacquer. Beginning of 18th c.

180.   Mirror framed in engraved glass and gilt wood. Beginning of
18th c.

181.   Mirror framed in black and gold lacquer. Beginning of 18th c.

182.   Mirror framed in gilt wood with bracket candlesticks. Beginning of 18th c.

183.   Mirror framed in gilt wood. Beginning of 18th c.

184.   Mirror framed in gilt wood and walnut. Beginning of 18th c.

185.   Mirror framed in gilt wood and glass. Beginning of 18th c.

186.   Secretary in yellow and green lacquer. Beginning of 18th c.

187.   Dressing table in satinwood. Late 18th c.

188.   Dressing table. Late 18th c.

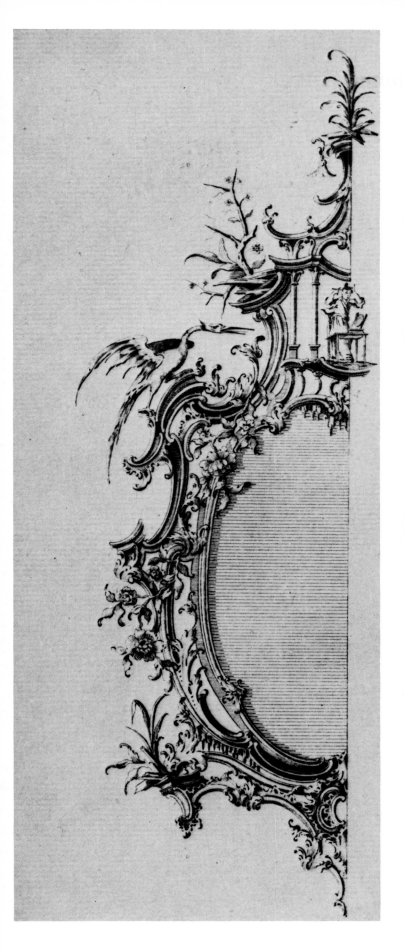

190.   Overmantel-mirror. Chippendale style.
Detail of pediment. 18th c.

189.   Sketch for the mirror illus. 192. Print by Chippendale.

191. Mirror framed in gilt wood. Chinese manner. Chippendale style. Middle of 18th c.

192. Detail of pediment in ▷ Ill. 191.

193. Dressing-case. Engraved glass and gold.
Beginning of 18th c.

194. Dance card. Gold and agate. Middle of 18th c.

196. Pocket-mirror. Gilt and silvered bronze. 18th c.

195. Dressing-case. Gold and red agate. About 1760.

197. Painted mirror with bevelled glass frame. 18th c.

198.   Mirror framed in cut glass. 18th c.

199. England. Girandole mirror in gilt wood. About 1800.

200. Mirror with engraved glass pediment. 18th c.

201. Mirror framed in painted wood and cut glass. Beginning of ▷ 19th c.

202.   Convex mirror. Gilt wood. Adam style. Beginning of 19th c.

203. U.S.A. Dressing table in walnut with mirror. 1870–80.

204. Mirror with iron frame and gold inlay. 16th c.

205. Mirror with mermaids. Gilt carving. 15th c.

206. Detail of the mirror
in Ill. 204.

208.   Mirror framed in gilt bronze. 16th c.

209, 210.   "Mermaid with Mirror". Jewellery. Attributed to Benvenuto Cellini. 1555.

211. Mirror with pedestal. Bronze and glass painted and gilded on reverse. 16th c.

212. Leonardo da Vinci's pocket-mirror in ivory and silver. 1500.

213.   Mirror framed in gilt wood. 18th c.

214.   Venice. Mirror with pediment. Cut glass. End of 18th c.

216.   Turin. Mirror with bracket candlesticks.
18th c.

217, 218. Genoa.
Mirror framed in gilt
wood and engraved
mirrors. 18th c.

221. Venice. Mirror framed in gilt wood decorated with engraved white and blue glass. 18th c.

222. Venice. Overmantel mirror. Gilt wood. 18th c.

223. Venice. Dressing-case. Blue lacquer. 18th c.

224. Venice. Mirrors framed in gilt wood and green lacquer. Chinese decoration. 18th c.

225. Monumental mirror with gilt polychorme frame. 18th c.

226.   Detail of mirror in Ill. 225

227.   Venice. Mirror framed in gilt wood and green lacquer. Chinese decoration. 18th c.

228.   Glass frame painted and gilded on reverse. 18th c.

229.   Mirror framed in Venetian glass. 18th c.   230.   Engraved mirror and gilt wood. 18th c.

232.   Gilt mirror. Blue
glass and rock-crystal.
18th c.

233. Venice. Mirror in yellow lacquer. 18th c.

234. Venice. Dressing-table mirror framed ▷
in lacquer. 18th c.

Following pages:
235, 236.   Mirror with pediment. Venetian
glass and engraving. End of 18th c.

237. Mirror framed in Venetian glass and engraved glass. 19th c.

238. Palermo. Chapel of the former ▷
Saint Philip's Monastery. Beginning of 18th c.

239, 240.   Palermo. Chapel of the former Saint-Philip's Monastery. Beginning of 18th c.

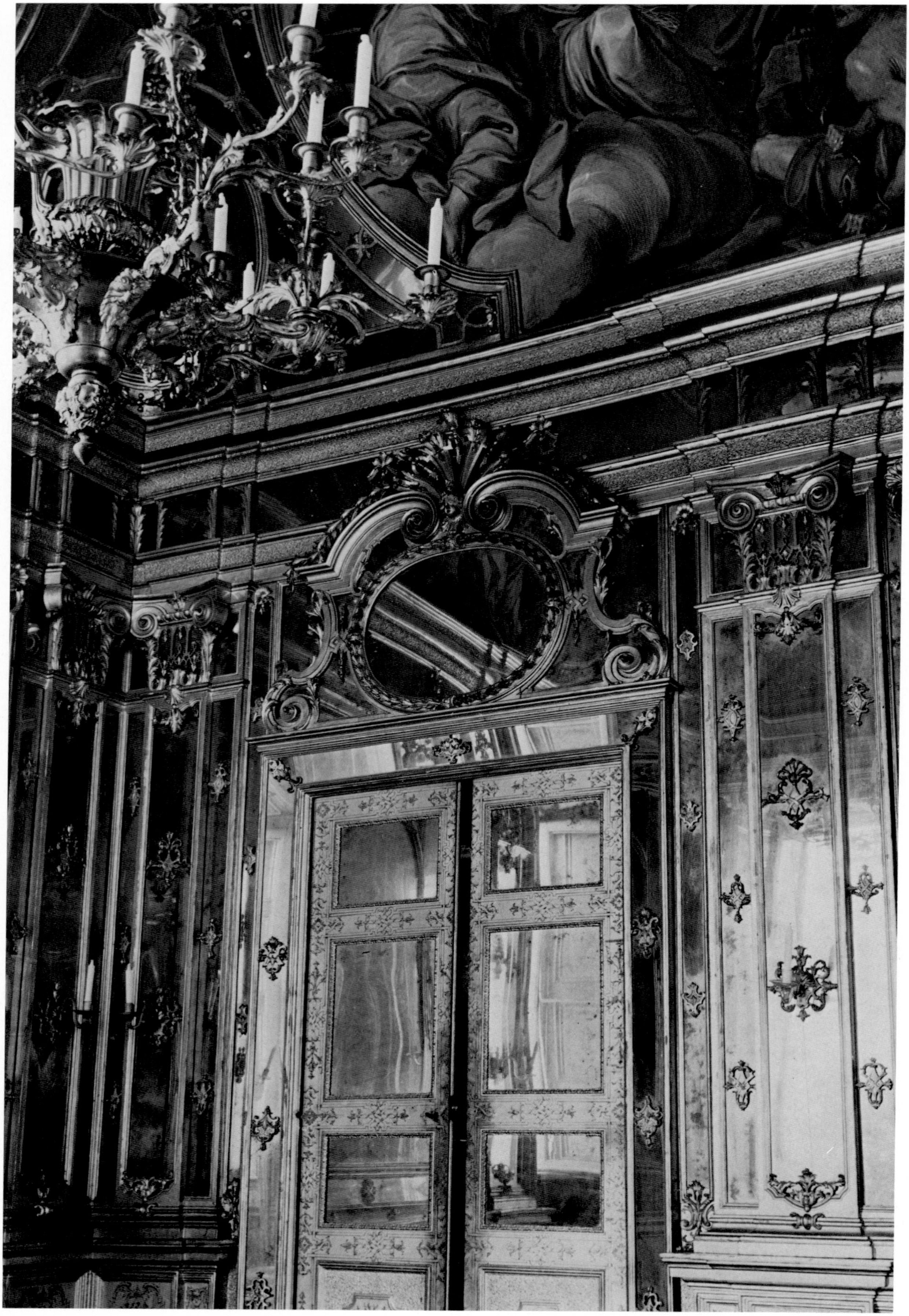

241–244. Bergamo. Palazzo Terzi. Gilt wood and mirrors. 18th c.

243. Bergamo.
Palazzo Terzi. Ceiling
decorated with mirrors,
gilt wood, and
frescoes. 18th c.

245. Isola Bella. Palazzo Borromeo. Chapel. 18th c.

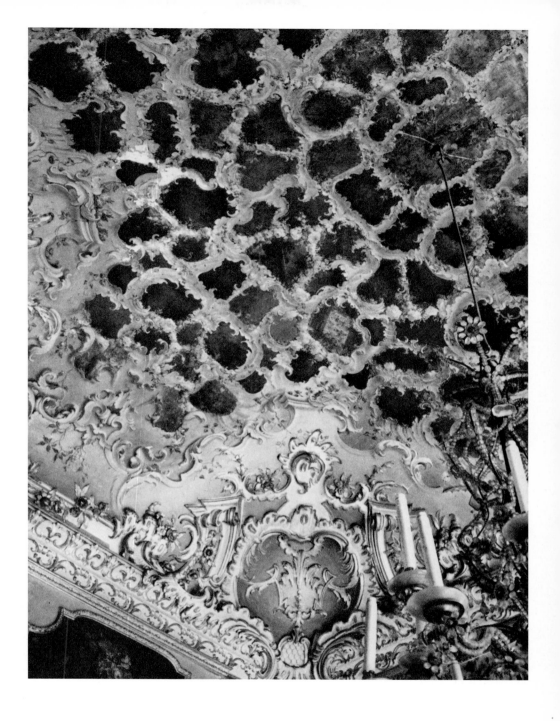

246. Royal castle of Stupinigi. Mirrors, stucco and gilt wood. 18th c.

186

248. Milan. Palazzo Litta. 18th c.

249, 250.   Guadalupe Convent. Bronze gilt mirror. Glass and rock-crystal. Beginning of 17th c.

251, 252.   Guadalupe Convent. Bronze gilt mirror. Glass and rock-crystal. Beginning of 17th c.

192

253. Guadalupe Convent. Sacristy. Decorated with carved wood and painted mirrors. 18th c.

254. Octagonal mirror. Gilt wood. Painted mirrors. Beginning of 17th c.

255. Mirror with gilt wood polychrome frame. Beginning of 18th c.

256. Gilt wood mirror decorated with small pieces of mirror surrounded by cemented hemp. Beginning of 18th c.

257, 258. Salamanca. Cathedral altar. Gilt frame and glass. 18th c.

259. Threefold mirror. Carved mahogany with inlay. End of 18th c.

260.   Dressing-case of tortoise-shell and silver. 18th c.

261–269.   Royal palace of Queluz.

261–263.   Throne room.

262.   Royal Palace of Queluz. Pilaster of the throne room.

264.   Royal Palace of Queluz. Detail of altar in gilt wood and glass. 18th c.

266. Royal Palace of Queluz. Detail of one
of the small drawing-rooms.

267. Royal Palace of Queluz. Pilaster of one
of the small drawing-rooms.

268. Royal Palace of Queluz. Detail of one of the small drawing-rooms.

269. Royal Palace of Queluz. Room of the queen. ▷

270. France. Wall mirror in limewood. About 1900.

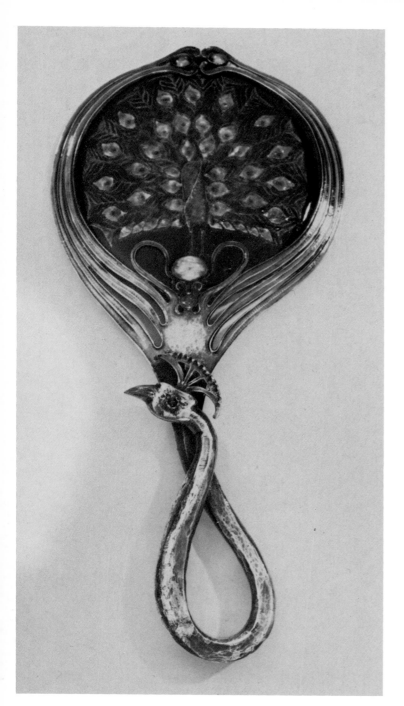

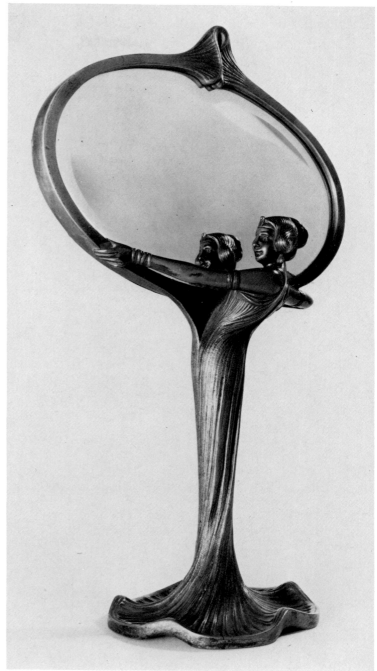

271. U.S.A. Hand-mirror in the stylized form of a peacock. About 1900.

272. England. Hand-mirror. By Webster. Picadilly. About 1900.

273.   France. Hand-mirror. By Henri Vever. 1889.

274.   France. Hand-mirror. By Henri Vever. Rear side. 1889.

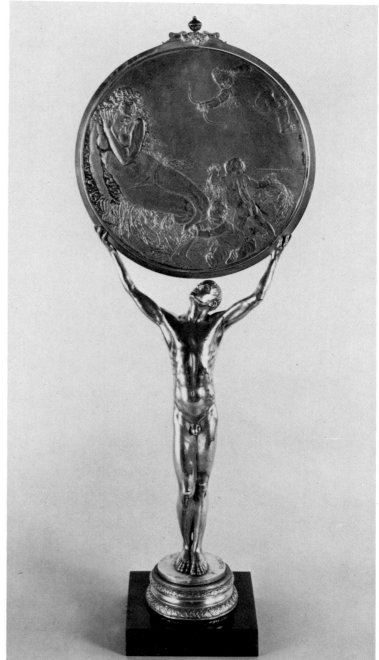

275.   France. Hand-mirror. By Henri Vever. 1889.

276.   Germany.   Hand-mirror. By Ernst Moritz Geyger. 1897.

278. France, Nancy. Mirror frame. By Louis Majorelle. About 1898.

277. France. Wardrobe with mirror doors. By Eugène Grasset. About 1900.

279. Holland. "The Vale of Tears". Carved wall mirror in untreated wood. By Barend Jordens. 1918.

280. U.S.A. Table mirror from the Tiffany studios. About 1900.

281. England. Mirror in silver. 1902–03.

282. Germany.
Dressing table.
By Richard
Riemerschmid. 1898.

283. Germany. Mirror frame in tin alloy.
About 1902.

284. Germany. Wall mirror. By Bernhard
Pankok. 1902.

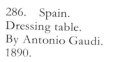

286. Spain.
Dressing table.
By Antonio Gaudi.
1890.

285. France. Wall mirror with console.
About 1900.

287. France.
Dressing table.
By Plumet and
Selmersheim.
About 1900.

213

288. Vienna. Dressing table. By Franz Messner. 1900.

289. Vienna. Full-length mirror. By Josef Hoffmann. About 1908.

290. Vienna. Sideboard. By Fritz Zeymer. About 1908.

291.   Vienna. Mirror frame. By Sigmund Jaray. About 1900.

292.   Austria. Mirror frame. By Franz Viehweider. 1901.

293.   Austria. Mirror frame. By Josef Hoffmann. Before 1928.

294.   Austria. Table mirror. By Josef Hoffmann. Before 1928.

295.   Austria. Mirror frame. By Josef Hoffmann. Before 1928.

296. Paris. Art Deco dining room. By Jules Leleu. 1925.

297. France. Interior design for living room with oval mirror. By Dominique and Alfred Porteneuve. 1925–30.

298.   France. Interior design with oval mirror. By Raymond Subes. 1925–30.

299.   France. Lacquered chest of drawers with oval mirror. By Paul Follot. 1925–30.

300. France. Chest of drawers in figwood with mirror. By Paul Follot. 1925–30.

301. France. "Les Jets d'Eau". Wrought-iron mirror by Edgar Brand. 1925.

302. France. Console and mirror in wrought iron. Nics Frères. 1925–30.

303. France. "Transition". Wall mirror in wrought iron. By Edgar Brandt. 1926.

304. France. Dressing table. By Armand Albert Rateau. 1920–22.

305. France. Toilet-mirror. By Armand Albert Rateau. 1920–22.

306. France. Cheval-glass in ebony. By Süe et Mare. 1925.

307. France. Sketch for a dressing table. By Jacques Ruhlmann. About 1927.

308. France. Dressing table in ebony. By Jacques Ruhlmann. About 1927.

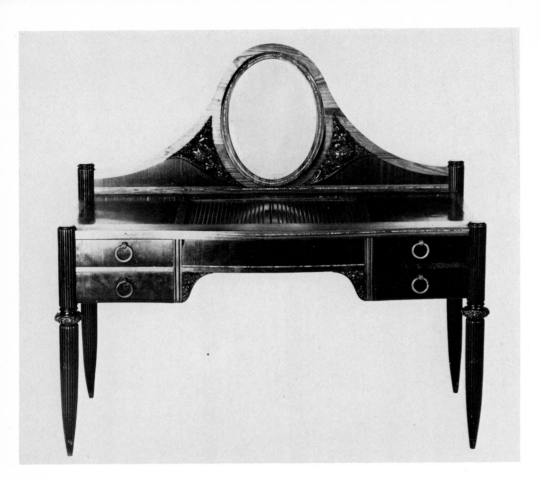

309.   France. Dressing table with oval mirror
By Maurice Dufrèsne. 1920–23.

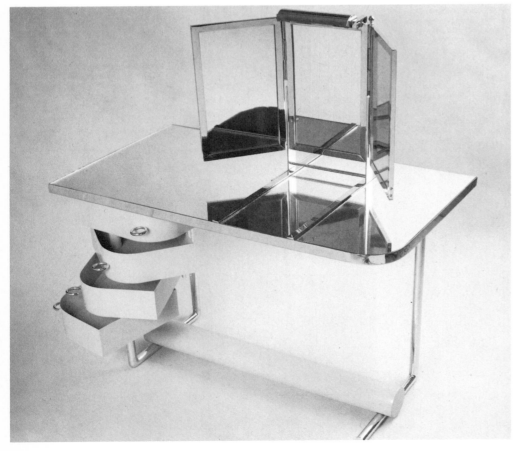

310.   France. Dressing table in chrome steel.
By René Herbst. 1930.

311. Fireplace with mirror panels. By Serge Roche. About 1934.

312. Sketch for console mirror. By Serge Roche. About 1934.

313.   Circular wall mirror with mirror-glass frame. By Serge Roche. 1930.

314.   Star-shaped mirror with mirror-glass frame. By Serge Roche. About 1934.

315.   Sun-shaped mirror with rays in mirror glass. 1930–1935.

316.   Pentagonal mirror in gilt and painted wood and plexiglass. By Mariano Andreü. 1930–35.